KU-515-153

Dear Helen,
dear Douglas,
thanks for the warm welcome
you gave us at your home

Uncle, Margot & Mare

August 1999

BERLIN

»Berlin ist dazu verdammt, immerfort zu werden und niemals zu sein.«

»Berlin is damned to constantly become and never to be.«

Karl Scheffler (Schriftsteller/author 1869–1951)

BERLIN

Jürgen Henkelmann
Volker Oesterreich

STÜRTZ VERLAG

INHALT

Ein Feuchtbiotop, auch
für Zweibeiner – Berlins
Pluspunkte sind die vielen
Wälder und grünen Lun-
gen wie der Tiergarten.

A damp biotope for crea-
tures great and small –
Berlin's plus points are its
many woods and green
spaces, such as Tiergarten
Park.

Seite 1: Beschwingt in der
Berliner Luft: die Flagge
des Stadtstaates mit dem
schwarzen Bären.

Page 1: Flapping happily
in the Berlin breeze:
the city state flag with its
black bear.

SUMMARY

Schattenspiel mit Prinz Albrecht von Preußen vor dem Charlottenburger Schloß-Turm.

Shadow play with Prince Albrecht of Prussia in front of the tower of Charlottenburg Palace.

Im Cinemascope-Format: das Uraufführungskino Zoo Palast am Breitscheidplatz.

In Cinemascope format: Berlin's »premiere« cinema, Zoo Palast, on Breitscheidplatz.

Leinen los: Berlin ist ein Dorado für Wassersportler, und nicht nur wie hier auf der Havel.

Letting loose: Berlin is an eldorado for watersports fanatics, and not just on the Havel River (shown here).

Von Zilles »Milljöh« zum High-Tech-Quartier

From Zille's »Milljöh« to the Hi-Tech Quarter

Seite 6: Symbol der Teilung, Symbol der Wiedervereinigung: Das Brandenburger Tor wurde 1788-91 am Pariser Platz erbaut.
Hier ging der letzte deutsche Kaiser beten: der Berliner Dom, im Vordergrund der Löwenkämpfer vor dem Alten Museum, entworfen von Christian Daniel Rauch, realisiert von Albert Wolff.

Page 6: A symbol of division and reunification: the Brandenburg Gate was built from 1788-91 on Pariser Platz.
The last German emperor's place of worship: Berlin Cathedral, with Christian Daniel Rauch's lion slayer in the foreground in front of the Old Museum.

Der Berliner Bär strotzt vor Kraft, fühlt sich aber dennoch schwach um die Brust. Nach der Wiedervereinigung mutierte er zum trunkenen Tanzbär, doch schon bald plagte ihn der Katzenjammer knapper Staatsfinanzen. Dem roten Adler Brandenburgs erging es kaum anders. Beide Wappentiere zeigten sich anlehnungsbedürftig und planten den Bund fürs Leben. Fusion hieß das (Auf-)-Gebot der Stunde. Doch das Wahlvolk verweigerte im Mai 1996 mehrheitlich die Trauzeugenschaft. Nun soll mit rund 200 Staatsverträgen eine Art wilde Ehe geschmiedet werden.

The Berlin bear is bursting with energy, yet feels a little out of pocket. The reunification turned him into a drunken dancing bear, who all too soon suffered the hangover of tight state finances. Brandenburg's red eagle underwent a similar fate. Both heraldic animals were feeling in need of care and support and decided to form a bond for life. Fusion, a marriage of needs, was what was called for. Yet in May 1996, the majority of the electorate refused to bear witness to the proposed happy event. Instead the two parties were offered a kind of common-law marriage involving approximately 200 state treaties.

Schwungvolle Geste: In der »Schwangeren Auster«, der Kongreßhalle, residiert heute das Haus der Kulturen der Welt.

A sweeping gesture: today, the »pregnant oyster« of the Congress Hall is home to the House of World Culture.

An Stuck wurde in der Gründerzeit nicht gespart: Fassaden-Schmuck am Kreuzberger Planufer.

Stucco was not something Gründerzeit architecture was short of: decorative façades on Kreuzberg's Planufer.

Linienbewußt: In Kreuzberg rattert die U-Bahn oberirdisch an der Heilig-Kreuz-Kirche vorbei.

Getting you there: in Kreuzberg, the Berlin Underground rattles overground past the Church of the Holy Cross.

Die Stadt an der Spree und an der Havel, an der Panke, Wuhle und Dahme geht dabei konsequent den Weg ins 21. Jahrhundert. Die Hauptstadt wird aus- und umgebaut, es herrscht eine Aufbruchsstimmung wie nach der Bismarckschen Reichsgründung 1871. Baukräne und Betonmischer markieren noch weit über das Jahr 2000 hinaus diese zweite Gründerzeit.

In keiner anderen Stadt Europas prallen Gestern, Heute und Morgen so unmittelbar aufeinander wie in Berlin. Zilles »Milljöh« ist wie anno tobak präsent, wenn der Kohlenmann mit gebündelten Briketts in die Keller steigt; gleichzeitig fühlt sich der Zeitgenosse beim Besuch im futuristischen ICC unterm Funkturm ins Raumschiff Enterprise gebeamt. Und während in so manchem morbiden Altbau-Kiez noch die Einschußlöcher in den Fassaden den Häuserkampf vom Ende des Zweiten Weltkriegs vergegenwärtigen, entsteht am Potsdamer Platz, mitten im Herzen der Stadt, ein Hightech-Quartier, wo bald 50 000 Menschen und mehr neue Jobs finden sollen. Dimensionen wie in Fritz Langs Stummfilmklassiker »Metropolis«.

Die Stadt atmet friederizianische Liberalität und Weltoffenheit. Das dunkelste deutsche Geschichtskapitel wird dagegen aufgeschlagen, wenn die NS-Monumentalarchitektur des alten Reichsluftfahrtministeriums an der Wilhelmstraße oder die davor freigelegten Fundamente der Gestapo-Zentrale zur Debatte stehen.

Die größten Chancen Berlins sehen viele in der Lage der Stadt, die sich mehr und mehr zur Drehscheibe zwischen Mittel- und Ost-Europa entwickelt. Von der östlichen Stadtgrenze sind es knapp 70 Kilometer

Despite this, the city on the Spree, Havel, Panke, Wuhle and Dahme rivers is entering the 21st century with vigour. The capital is being rebuilt and extended; a sense of departure is in the air, akin to that felt after Bismarck's foundation of the German Reich in 1871. Cranes and cement mixers will mark Berlin's second Gründerzeit long after the year 2000 has passed.

There is no other city in Europe where yesterday, today and tomorrow collide with such force. In Berlin, Zille's »Milljöh« is as present as in the year dot when the coalman goes down into the cellar carrying a bundle of briquettes; yet at the same time, contemporaries feel as if they have just been beamed up aboard the Starship Enterprise when visiting the futuristic International Congress Centre under the radio tower. Whereas in some older districts, the shell holes in the morbid façades make the final battles in and around the houses at the end of World War II barely seem a thing of the past, a hi-tech quarter is emerging on Potsdamer Platz, in the heart of the city, where soon over 50,000 people will find new jobs. These are dimensions reminiscent of Fritz Lang's classic silent film, »Metropolis«.

The city breathes Frederickian liberality and cosmopolitan attitudes. The darkest chapter in Germany's history will, however, soon been reopened when the monumental architecture of the Third Reich's Imperial Air Ministry in the Wilhelmstraße or the unearthed foundations of the Gestapo headquarters in front of it are put up for debate.

Many consider Berlin's greatest asset to be the city's location, increasingly becoming a turntable between Cen-

Ruinen-Charme: Im Hinterhof des Kulturzentrums Tacheles im Bezirk Mitte.

Charm of ruins: in the courtyard of Tachele arts centre in the Mitte district.

Luftlinie bis nach Polen. Schon jetzt kommen viele von dort zum Einkaufen an die Spree. Auch auf die Russen übt Berlin eine magische Anziehungskraft aus. Sie fühlen sich in Charlottenburg oder Lichtenberg fast schon so zu Hause wie in Minsk oder St. Petersburg. Das war schon einmal so, während der Roaring Twenties, als gut 200 000 Russen infolge der Oktoberrevolution an der Spree ihr Exil suchten. Damals benannten die Berliner ihr Charlottenburg kurzerhand in Charlottengrad um.

Der multikulturelle Schmelztiegel erhält seine besonderen Farbtupfer freilich auch durch den hohen türkischen Bevölkerungsanteil, insbesondere in den Bezirken Wedding, Kreuzberg, Tiergarten und Neukölln. Die 140 000 türkischen Berliner könnten glatt eine eigene Großstadt bevölkern.

Wichtigste Trumpfkarte im Ärmel ist jedoch die Kulturszene mit ihren unendlich vielen Facetten. Drei Opernhäuser von Weltrang wetteifern in Berlin um die Gunst des Publikums. Die Philharmoniker und sieben wei-

tral and Eastern Europe. There are only about 70 kilometres between the city's eastern boundaries and Poland. Many Poles already come shopping on the Spree River. Berlin also seems to exert a magical drawing force over Russians. They feel just as at home in Charlottenburg or Lichtenberg as they do in Minsk or St. Petersburg. This is nothing new; in the Roaring Twenties, a good 200,000 Russians sought exile on the Spree after the October Revolution, causing Berlin residents to rename Charlottenburg »Charlottengrad«.

The multicultural melting pot wouldn't been complete without Berlin's large Turkish population, mainly concentrated in the Wedding, Kreuzberg, Tiergarten and Neukölln districts. The 140,000 Turkish inhabitants are enough to populate their own large city.

Yet Berlin's trump card must be its broad span of cultural offerings. Three world-famous opera houses vie for custom. The Berlin Philharmonic and seven other top orchestras regularly beat their timpani with brilliance

Kalte Dusche: An heißen Sommertagen bietet der »Wasserklops« vor dem Europa Center eine willkommene Abkühlung.

A cold shower: the Wasserklops globe fountain in front of the Europa-Center is a good place to cool off on a hot summer's day.

Zwei Kopftücher, zwei Welten: In der Kreuzberger Oranienstraße präsentiert sich das multikulturelle Berlin am anschaulichsten.

Two headscarves for two different worlds: Berlin is at its most cosmopolitan in Kreuzberg's Oranienstraße.

tere Spitzenorchester hauen mal fulminant auf die Pauke, mal streichen sie feinfühlig die Saiten. Mehr als 150 Museen locken mit Saurier-Gebein oder den Farbexplosionen der Jungen Wilden, mit dem Pergamonaltar oder einem Verbrecheralbum aus dem Jahre 1876. Und auf 20 großen und vielen, vielen kleinen Bühnen wird der Literatur theatralisch Leben eingehaucht.

Das Brandenburger Tor, 1791 nach den Entwürfen von Carl Gotthard Langhans vollendet, steht als Symbol für alles zusammen: für die Geschichte und Gegenwart, für Napoleon, Kaiser Wilhelm II., Hitler und Gorbatschow, die alle Berlin ihren Stempel aufgedrückt haben; es steht für die mondänen Villen von Grunewald oder die tristen Plattensilos von Marzahn. Zu Mauerzeiten Mahnmal der Konfrontation zweier Machtblöcke, wird das

or bow strings with sensitivity. More than 150 museums lure visitors with dinosaur skeletons or the colourful artistic explosions of the Junge Wilden (A. R. Penck and co.), with the Pergamon Altar or an album of crimes from 1876. And on 20 large and numerous small stages, literature has theatrical life breathed into it.

The Brandenburg Gate, completed in 1791 from plans by Carl Gotthard Langhans, is a symbol of everything together, of the past and present, of Napoleon, Emperor William II, Hitler and Gorbachov, all of whom have left their mark on Berlin; it is a symbol of Grunewald's elegant villas or Marzahn's sad, concrete-slab tower blocks. While the Wall still stood, it was a memorial to the confrontation between two power blocs; now it is a monument to the reunification. When the Brandenburg Gate was opened

Seite 10/11: Über diese Brücke muß er gehen: Die Tiergartenbrücke führt den Bundespräsidenten direkt zu seinem Amtssitz, dem Schloß Bellevue. Die Baustelle wird zur Schaustelle: Am Potsdamer Platz werden Milliarden in das neue Berlin investiert.

Page 10/11: This is one bridge he definitely has to cross: Tiergarten Bridge leads the German president straight to his new seat of office, Bellevue Palace. From building site to showpiece: billions are being invested in the new Berlin on Potsdamer Platz.

Wannsee-Visite: An der Terrasse von Heckeshorn beginnt einer der idyllischsten Spazier- und Radwege entlang des Wassers.

A visit to Wannsee Lake: one of the idyllic footpaths and cycle paths along the water's edge starts at this Heckeshorn terrace.

Brandenburger Tor heute als Monument der Wiedervereinigung interpretiert. Als sich der »antifaschistische Schutzwall« an dieser Stelle zwei Tage vor Heiligabend 1989 für die Massen öffnete, lagen sich unter Schadows Quadriga Ost und West in den Armen. Unvergeßlich für alle, die

for the masses three days before Christmas in 1989, East and West fell into each other's arms under Schadow's Quadriga. It was an event which will never be forgotten by those who were there.

Auf der schloßherrlichen Schokoladenseite von Schloß Charlottenburg verdoppeln sich die maßvollen 500 Meter des preußischen Barocks im Spiegelbild auf einen Kilometer.

In the lake at Charlottenburg Palace, the modest 500 metres of glorious Prussian Baroque are doubled in their mirror image to one kilometre.

DIE HAUPTSTADT – DAMALS UND HEUTE

Prägende Figur der preußisch-deutschen Machtpolitik: Bismarck-Denkmal im Bezirk Tiergarten.

An imposing figure in Prussian-German power politics: the Bismarck Monument in the Tiergarten district.

Bundespräsident Richard von Weizsäcker hatte die Nase vorn. Als erster Repräsentant des Staates verlegte er seinen Amtssitz 1994 von Bonn ins Berliner Schloß Bellevue. Zur Jahrtausendwende sollen Parlament und Regierung folgen. Eine umstrittene Entscheidung, zumal die reinen Umzugskosten auf rund 20 Milliarden Mark geschätzt werden. Rasch formierte sich die Berlin-Opposition: zum einen, weil man wirtschaftliche Nachteile für die Bonner Region befürchtet; zum anderen, weil eine große Zahl von Regierungsbediensteten den Wechsel aus privaten Gründen scheut. Gegen Berlin als Regierungssitz wurde oft mit historisch belegten Argumenten polemisiert. Die Stadt an der Spree könne – von der stets umkämpften Weimarer Republik einmal abgesehen – auf keine große demokratische Tradition verweisen, hieß es. Das ist richtig, wenn man an den NS-Terror denkt, der von der Wilhelmstraße aus gelenkt wurde. Weder die Worte Kaiser Wilhelms II., der den damals neuen Reichstag als »Reichsaffenhaus« diffamierte, stehen auf dem Büttenpapier der Geschichtsschreibung, noch erweist sich der Rückblick auf Berlin als »Hauptstadt der DDR« als Ruhmesblatt. Andererseits steht die Spree-Metropole auch für den Widerstand gegen das Hitler-Regime. Der friedliche Umbruch in der DDR hatte in Berlin seine Wurzeln, und in den Westsektoren hielt man nach 1945 sehr wohl das Fähnlein der Demokratie ganz weit nach oben - mit alliierter Schützenhilfe. Alles in allem erscheint der Regierungsumzug mehr als konsequent. Kaum hatte der Verpackungskünstler Christo an Paul Wallots Reichstags-gebäude seine Hüllen fallengelassen, da begann schon im Sommer 1995 der Umbau für den Deutschen Bundestag. Der britische Stararchitekt Sir Norman Foster bringt das Parlament im wahrsten Sinne des Wortes unter die (gläserne) Haube, und zwar in freier Interpretation von Wallots alter Kuppel. 1999 soll alles fertig sein. Im Umkreis werden nach und nach die Abgeordneten-Büros und Ministerien bezugsfertig – fast alle in renovierten Altbauten. Spektakulärster Regierungsneubau ist der sogenannte Schultes-Riegel nach Plänen der Architekten Axel Schultes und Charlotte Frank. Kern des Gebäudekomplexes wird

Kleine Berlin-Statistik

Mit rund 3,5 Millionen Einwohnern ist Berlin die mit Abstand größte deutsche Stadt. Knapp zwei Millionen davon leben in den ehemaligen West-Bezirken. Die Gesamtfläche beträgt 889 Quadratkilometer, darin fände fast das gesamte Ruhrgebiet Platz. Mehr als ein Drittel machen Wald, Wasser-, und Grünflächen aus. Wer von Wannsee nach Buch oder von Frohnau nach Rahnsdorf einmal diagonal durch Berlin fährt, braucht mit dem Auto dafür mindestens eineinhalb Stunden und legt beide Male rund 40 Kilometer zurück. Berlin besteht aus 23 Bezirken mit jeweils einem Bezirksbürgermeister an der Spitze. Durch Zusammenlegung soll die Zahl demnächst auf 18 reduziert werden. Chef der Landesregierung ist der Regierende Bürgermeister mit Sitz im Roten Rathaus. Das Abgeordnetenhaus tagt im ehemaligen Preußischen Landtag. Berlin ist auch eine bedeutende Industrie- und Wissenschaftsstadt. An den 18 Hoch- und Fachhochschulen sind derzeit rund 135 000 Studenten immatrikuliert.

das Bundeskanzleramt sein. Gut einen Kilometer entfernt schlummern die Überreste von Hitlers Reichskanzlei im Erdreich...

oben: Hier zieht nach der Renovierung der Deutsche Bundestag ein: das Reichstagsgebäude. unten: Hier stand der Schreibtisch von Erich Honecker: das Staatsratsgebäude im Bezirk Mitte.

above: The Reichstag will be the German Bundestag's new home once renovation is complete. below: This is where Erich Honecker once sat at his desk: the GDR head of state building in Mitte.

THE CAPITAL –
THEN AND NOW

German president Richard von Weizsäcker was one step ahead of everyone else. As the first representative of the state, he moved his seat of office from Bonn to Berlin's Bellevue Palace in 1994. Parliament and government are to follow for the next millennium. Weizsäcker's decision is a controversial one, as just the moving costs are estimated at ca. 20 billion German marks. Opposition to the Berlin move has grown rapidly, on the one hand as it is feared that the Bonn region will suffer economic disadvantage because of it, and on the other because a large number of government officials are shrinking back from the change for private reasons. Historically verified arguments have often been inveighed against Berlin as the seat of government. One claims that the city on the River Spree – ignoring the terminally disputed Weimar Republic – has never demonstrated any great democratic tradition. This is true when we think back to the National Socialists' reign of terror, directed from the Wilhelmstraße. Nor have William II's words, proclaiming the then new Reichstag the »State Monkey House«, earned themselves pride of place in the history books, and Berlin as the »capital of the German Democratic Republic« can also not be counted among the city's better days.
One must not forget, however, that the metropolis on the Spree also symbolises resistance to the Hitler regime. The peaceful change in the GDR had its roots in Berlin, and after 1945 the flag of democracy was held high in the west sectors, – albeit with the help of Allied soldiers.
All in all, the government's move to Berlin seems more than rigorous. Hardly had packaging artist Christo's

Historisch: Das Museum im Zeughaus zeugt von der deutschen Geschichte.

Historical: the museum in the old Arsenal is a witness to German history.

wrappings been removed from Paul Wallot's Reichstag, than rebuilding began in the summer of 1995 for the German Bundestag. British star architect, Sir Norman Foster, will (architecturally at least) be subjecting the government to the »greenhouse effect«; his new glass design for the building is a free interpretation of Wallot's original dome. Completion is scheduled for 1999.

Berlin - Some Statistics

With 3.5 million inhabitants, Berlin is by far the largest city in Germany. Almost two million people alone live in what used to be the west sectors. Berlin's surface area totals 889 square kilometres, almost enough room for the entire Ruhr area. Forest, water and green spaces make up more than one third of this. Travelling diagonally across Berlin from Wannsee to Buch or from Frohnau to Rahnsdorf by car will take you at least one-and-a-half hours and cover about 40 kilometres on each route.

Berlin has 23 districts each run by a district mayor. This number is to be reduced to 18 in future by merging several of the districts. The head of provincial government is the Mayor of Berlin with a seat of office in the Red Town Hall. The House of Representatives sits in the former Prussian Landtag.
Berlin is also an important industrial and economic centre. Approximately 135,000 students are currently enrolled at its 18 universities and colleges.

One by one, the surrounding offices and ministries are being made ready for their new tenants – almost all are in restored old buildings. The most spectacular new government building is the so-called »Schultes-Riegel«, designed by architects Axel Schultes and Charlotte Frank.
The Federal Chancellery will form the centrepiece of the building complex. A good kilometre away, the remains of Hitler's chancellery, the Reichskanzlei, slumber under the ground.

Hier läßt's sich leben und repräsentieren: Schloß Bellevue in Tiergarten, der Amts- und Wohnsitz des Bundespräsidenten.

Living, working and representing the state: Bellevue Palace in Tiergarten, residence and seat of office to the president of Germany.

15

Seite 18/19: Debattierclub: Erst schnürten Christo und Jeanne-Claude ihr kunstvolles Päckchen, dann begannen die Umbauarbeiten, damit die Bundestagsabgeordneten ihr Ränzlein schnüren können – unterwegs nach Berlin.
Seite 16/17: In weiter Ferne, so nah: Durch das Teleobjektiv rücken die Wahrzeichen von Ost und West entlang der Achse Schloßbrücke – Unter den Linden – Straße des 17. Juni nah zueinander.

Page 18/19: Debating society: first it was the turn of Christo and wife Jeanne-Claude to tighten the ropes around their wrapped package. Then renovation work began, and now members of parliament have to start packing their bags for the move to Berlin.
Page 16/17: So far and yet so near: the zoom lens shrinks the distance between the symbols of East and West Berlin along the axis of Schloßbrücke, Unter den Linden and the Straße der 17. Juni.

18

Nach der Sanierung durch Sir Norman Foster soll auch wieder eine gläserne Kuppel in Form eines halbierten Eis Paul Wallots alten Parlamentsbau krönen.

After Sir Norman Foster's restoration work has been completed, a glass dome shaped like half an egg shall once again surmount Paul Wallot's old parliament building.

Mit Heine mitten durch die Mitte

Straight Through the Middle of Berlin with Heine

Heinrich Heine traf den Nagel auf den Kopf. In seinen »Briefen aus Berlin« beschrieb der junge Dichter 1822 sehr genau die Atmosphäre der preußischen Residenzstadt. Er kolportierte den Klatsch aus Opernhaus und Cafés, hörte Vorlesungen von Hegel und Savigny und traf im literarischen Salon der Rahel Varnhagen die geistige Elite seiner Epoche.

Besonders angetan war Heine von der Flaniermeile unter den Linden: »Hier drängt sich Prachtgebäude an Prachtgebäude«, schwärmte er, um gleich darauf vom genügsamen König zu plaudern, der zwei- statt sechsspännig durch die Stadt kutschierte.

Heinrich Heine hit the nail right on the head. In 1822 in his »Letters from Berlin«, the young poet very accurately described the atmosphere prevalent in the Prussian royal capital. He peddled the latest gossip from the opera house and cafés, attended lectures by Hegel and Savigny and met up with the intellectual elite of his day and age in Rahel Varnhagen's literary salon.

Heine was especially impressed by the avenue Unter den Linden. »Magnificent building flanks magnificent building«, he enthuses, only to then chatter on about the modest king who rides through the city on a

Seite 20: Wem die Stunde schlägt: Die Weltzeituhr am Alexanderplatz tickt auch für Übersee ganz richtig.

Page 20: For whom the bell tolls: the World Time Clock on Alexanderplatz also ticks for overseas countries.

Charme und Geschicklichkeit heißen die beiden Trumpfkarten beim Gauklerfest vor der Kulisse der Friedrichwerderschen Kirche - faszinierend auch für junges Publikum.

Skill and charm is what's called for when entertaining even the smallest of onlookers in front of Friedrichswerder Church.

coach pulled by two and not six horses.

Witnesses in stone to this old Berlin are still evident between the Brandenburg Gate and the Schloßbrücke. From the dome of Berlin Cathedral (consecrated only in 1905), an exhibit of Wilhelminian exhibitionism with great architectural gesture, it is possible to detect the flair Heine was referring to. Classical façades (original or imitation) are in abundance. Posh limousines pull up in front of the Staatsoper when Harry Kupfer and Daniel Barenboim stage Wagner's »Ring«. The Baroque Arsenal gleams in its new coat of old rose, home to the collection of the German Historical Museum. The empty bookshelves set into the ground on Opernplatz remind us of the Nazi book burnings – right opposite the two Humboldt statues in front of the university. Between them, Old Fritz (Frederick II) rides his favourite horse, Condé, in bronze, as if not the slightest bit interested in the modern army of cars circling round him.

Only the old City Palace is missing from the picture; on the orders of head of state Walter Ulbricht, its war-ravaged ruins were demolished in the Fifties. A single portal remains, from whence Karl Liebknecht called for a Socialist republic in 1918. It now adorns the façade of the former Council of State building on the south side of Schloßplatz.

Almost exactly where the City Palace once stood, the Palace of the Republic was erected for the East German parliament in the Seventies. After years of squabbling over its future, it is to be finally pulled down, with the exception of the chamber (a listed historical monument) where the last GDR parliament agreed to join the

Aus internationaler Sicht das bekannteste deutsche Theater: das Berliner Ensemble. Bertolt Brecht und Helene Weigel spuken noch immer durchs Haus. Begraben liegen sie auf dem Dorotheenstädtischen Friedhof.

Berlin's best-known theatre all over the world: the Berliner Ensemble. Bertolt Brecht and Helene Weigel still haunt these revered walls. They are buried in the Dorotheenstadt cemetery.

Steinerne Zeugnisse dieses alten Berlins existieren zwischen Brandenburger Tor und Schloßbrücke nach wie vor. Vom Kuppelumgang des (allerdings erst 1905 eingeweihten) Doms, der mit großer architektonischer Geste das wilhelminische Imponiergehabe attestiert, läßt sich das Flair von damals sehr gut nachvollziehen. Klassizistische Fassaden (original oder epigonal) gibt's zuhauf. Vor der Staatsoper halten Nobelkarossen, wenn Harry Kupfer und Daniel Barenboim zum Wagnerschen »Ring«-Zyklus bitten. Das barocke Zeughaus erstrahlt in neuem Alt-Rosa und beherbergt die Sammlung des Deut-

Frisch vergoldet: die Kuppeln der Neuen Synagoge an der Oranienburger Straße.

Freshly gilded: the dome of the New Synagogue in Oranienburger Straße.

schen Historischen Museums. Am Opernplatz erinnern die im Boden eingelassenen leeren Regale an die Bücherverbrennung der Nazis – genau vis à vis der beiden Humboldt-Standbilder vor der Universität. Dazwischen reitet der Alte Fritz in Bronze auf seinem Lieblingspferd »Condé«, als ginge ihn die neuzeitliche Blechlawine ringsum gar nichts an.

Bloß das Stadtschloß fehlt in der Mitte; seine Kriegsruine wurde in den fünfziger Jahren auf Geheiß des Genossen Staatsratsvorsitzenden Walter Ulbricht gesprengt. Ein einziges Portal blieb erhalten: das, von

Federal Republic. This chamber is to be integrated into a new building, with an imitation of the old palace façade stuck on its front. If Heine were still alive, he would surely have a literary witticism to hand, both on this new castle in the air and on »Erich's lamp shop«, as the Palace of the Republic is called in reference to former Socialist leader, Erich Honecker.

While Heine was in Berlin, Karl Friedrich Schinkel was brooding over the first plans for the Old Museum. The columned building opened in 1830 was the first of the strange ensemble to develop over the next 100 years on

Orthodoxe unter sich: Vor dem Holocaust waren solche Szenen an der Tagesordnung im alten Scheunenviertel.

Orthodox Jews: these were common scenes in the old Scheunenviertel before the Holocaust.

dem Karl Liebknecht 1918 die sozialistische Republik ausrief. Nun ziert es die Fassade des ehemaligen Staatsratsgebäudes an der Südseite des Schloßplatzes.

Fast genau an der Stelle des ehemaligen Stadtschlosses wurde in den siebziger Jahren der Palast der Republik für die DDR-Volkskammer errichtet. Nach jahrelangem Hickhack über dessen Zukunft wird der »Palazzo

Berlin's museum island. It houses treasures such as the Pergamon Altar, art from Late Antiquity and the Byzantine period, and immense creative riches from Renoir to Liebermann. They will soon be joined by Egyptian queen Nefertiti, moving from Charlottenburg in the wake of the large-scale reorganisation of the collection. To this end, the New Museum, heavily damaged in the last

Bevölkerung von Berlin / Number of Inhabitants			
1600	9.000		
1719	64.000		
1816	223.000		
1880	1.321.000		
1895	2.269.960		
1905	3.226.049	**Berlin-West**	**Berlin-Ost**
1925	4.024.458	**Berlin-West**	**Berlin-East**
1942	4.478.102		
1945	2.807.405	1.733.606	1.073.799
1955	3.343.182	2.203.318	1.139.864
1975	3.083.011	1.984.837	1.098.174
1993	3.475.393		

Protzo« nun abgerissen - mit Ausnahme des denkmalgeschützten Plenarsaals, in dem das letzte DDR-Parlament den Beitritt zur Bundesrepublik beschlossen hat. Dieser Rest soll in einen Neubau integriert werden, an den womöglich eine Imitation der alten Schloßfassade gepappt wird. Lebte Heine noch, er hätte bestimmt eine literarische Sottise parat – sowohl über das Luftschloß als auch über »Erichs Lampenladen«, wie der Palast der Republik in Anspielung auf den ehemaligen SED-Chef Erich Honecker auch genannt wird.

Während Heine in Berlin weilte, grübelte Karl Friedrich Schinkel schon über die ersten Entwürfe für das Alte Museum. Der 1830 eröffnete Säulenbau bildete den Auftakt jenes einzigartigen Ensembles, das in den folgenden 100 Jahren auf der Museumsinsel entstand. Es beherbergt Schätze wie

war, has to be restored and extended. At the beginning of the 19th century, Heine was also fascinated by the Friedrichstraße. »One can imagine the notion of eternity when looking at this [street]«. At its south end, between Checkpoint Charlie and Unter den Linden, it rapidly became an eldorado for large-scale investors after the Wall came down. A billion-mark monopoly was staged around

Backsteinfassade und Kupferkuppel: Das alte Postfuhramt an der Oranienburger Straße soll zum Museum werden (oben). Die St.-Hedwigs-Kathedrale (unten), Hauptkirche des Bistums Berlin, wurde 1747 nach dem Vorbild des römischen Pantheons erbaut.

Brick façade and copper dome: the old Post Office in Oranienburger Straße is to be turned into a museum (top).
St. Hedwig's Cathedral (bottom), the main church of the diocese of Berlin, was built in 1747 and modelled on the Pantheon in Rome.

Neues Leben im alten Stadtquartier: das Café Orange an der Oranienburger Straße.

New life in an old part of town: the Café Orange in Oranienburger Straße.

Vor- und Nachleser:
Zu Füßen von Wilhelm
von Humboldt gibt's
antiquarisches Studenten-
futter aus Bananenkar-
tons. Anschließend wird
die geistige Nahrung in
der *Alma mater* Unter den
Linden verdaut.

The world of books at
Wilhelm von Humbolt's
feet: looking for second-
hand academic fodder
in old banana boxes.
The contents are digested
in the new owner's *alma
mater* in Unter den
Linden.

Hier wurde 1990 der
Einigungsvertrag zwi-
schen beiden deutschen
Staaten unterschrieben:
das Kronprinzenpalais
Unter den Linden.

This is where the unification treaty between the
two German states was
signed in 1990: the
Crown Prince's Palace in
Unter den Linden.

den Pergamon-Altar, spätantike und byzantinische Kunst sowie unermeß-liche schöpferische Reichtümer von Renoir bis Liebermann. Bald zieht auch Nofretete von Charlottenburg auf die Museumsinsel – im Zuge der großangelegten Neuordnung der Sammlungen. Voraussetzung dafür sind Restaurierung und Erweite-rung des kriegszerstörten Neuen Museums.

Fasziniert war Heine Anfang des 19. Jahrhunderts auch von der Friedrich-straße: »Wenn man diese betrachtet, kann man sich die Idee der Unend-lichkeit veranschaulichen.« Im süd-lichen Teil, zwischen Checkpoint Charlie und Unter den Linden, avan-cierte sie nach dem Mauerfall zum Dorado für Großinvestoren. Ein wah-res Milliarden-Monopoly wurde um die mondäne Friedrichstadtpassage veranstaltet. Noch pompöser wirkt

the fashionable Friedrichstadt pre-cinct. Even more pompous is the building site of the century on Pots-damer Platz, previously a Wall no-man's land, where multinationals such as Daimler Benz, Sony, ABB and the Deutsche Bahn are slogging away for all they are worth. By the year 2002, eight billion German marks will have been pumped into fancy office blocks and functional tunnels.

Die erste Adresse auf der Museumsinsel: Eingang zum Pergamonmuseum.

The number one address on Berlin's museum island: the entrance to the Pergamon Museum.

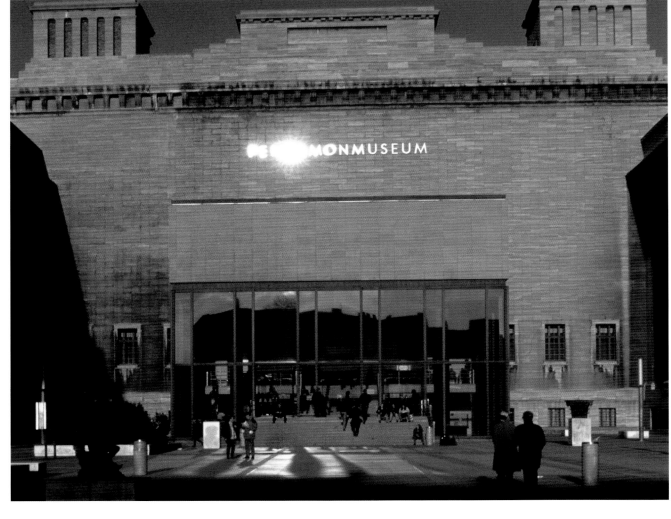

Prunkstück: Vor dem Pergamonaltar huldigte man um 150 vor Christus dem Götterpaar Zeus und Athene. 1902 kam er aus der Türkei nach Berlin.

The museum's showpiece: around 150 years B.C., worshippers to the gods Zeus and Athena regularly prostrated themselves before the Pergamon Altar, brought to Berlin from Turkey in 1902.

die Jahrhundert-Baustelle an der früheren Mauer-Brache des Potsdamer Platzes, wo Multis wie Daimler Benz, Sony, ABB und die Deutsche Bahn klotzen, was das Zeug hält. Acht Milliarden Mark verwandeln sich dort bis zum Jahre 2002 in schicke Büropaläste und funktionale Tunnels.

Nördlich der Linden wurde unterdessen der gläserne »Tränenpalast« am Bahnhof Friedrichstraße zum Party- und Pop-Schuppen umfunktioniert. Die Ironie der Geschichte will es, daß dort, wo einst die Grenzer die aus Ost-Berlin ausreisenden Touristen filzten, nun eine Combo wie »Die Zöllner« zur phonstarken Trommelfell-Attacke aufmarschieren kann.

Überhaupt hat die Friedrichstraße in dieser Gegend die Muse geküßt. Im Metropol-Theater entführt René Kollo seine Klientel operettenselig ins

At the north end of Unter den Linden, the glass »palace of tears« at Friedrichstraße Station has been turned into a party and pop dive. The irony of history is such that where border guards once frisked tourists leaving East Berlin, groups with names such as »The Customs Officials« are now allowed to launch high-level decibel attacks on unsuspecting eardrums, tourist or otherwise.

Das »Museumsschiff« und der Ausflugsdampfer auf der Spree: Das Bodemuseum bildet den Bug der Museumsinsel, die für Hunderte von Millionen restauriert, ausgebaut und konzeptionell neu gestaltet werden soll.

The »museum-ship« and the pleasure steamer on the Spree: the Bode Museum is the bow of museum island, restored, extended and redesigned for hundreds of millions of German marks.

»Land des Lächelns«, und in der »Distel« offeriert man den Zuschauern kabarettistische Pralinés mit (n)ostalgischer Senffüllung. Selbst die Weidendammer Brücke über die Spree bietet Stoff für poetische Höhenflüge. Wolf Biermann besang die gußeisernen Adler im Brückengeländer, und zwar ganz in Heinescher Manier. Von dort aus hatte der Liedermacher auch das Berliner Ensemble im Blick, einst sein Arbeitsplatz. Die Tradition von Bertolt Brecht und Heiner Müller führt nun der Schauspieler Martin Wuttke mit neuen Akzenten fort. Als Intendant spuken ihm freilich immer noch die

Die Ruinen-Bohème frönt ihrer bizarren Schrott-Ästhetik hinter dem Kunsthaus Tacheles, ein tägliches Happening an der Oranienburger Straße.

Behind the Tachele arts centre, the ruin bohemia indulge in their bizarre junk art, a daily occurrence in Oranienburger Straße.

ehrenwerten »Hausgeister« des Berliner Ensembles durch den Kopf. Sollte ihm die Last der Vergangenheit zu schwer werden, kann er sich von der Konkurrenz im nahen Deutschen Theater auf andere Gedanken bringen lassen. Vielleicht zieht es Wuttke zur Ablenkung sogar in den neuen Friedrichstadtpalast, der mit den 62 schönsten Beinen von Berlin

The Friedrichstraße in this area seems to be a general source of inspiration to artistes of all calibres. In the Metropol-Theatre, René Kollo whisks his clientele away into the »Land of Smiles« on an operatic cloud, and in the Distle (thistle) the audience are offered cabaret chocolates with nostalgic, »GDR« mustard centres. Even the Weidendammbrücke over the Spree produces material for poetic flights of fancy. Wolf Biermann sang an ode to the cast-iron eagles on the parapet in true Heine style. From his make-shift stage, the singer-songwriter had an excellent view of the Berliner Ensem-

oben: Original und Fälschung: Die Schloßbrückenfiguren sind historisch, die Fassadenattrappe dahinter existierte nur vorübergehend (rechts).
unten: Als wär's im Orient: Auf dem Flohmarkt neben der Tacheles-Ruine wird Tausendundallerlei verhökert.

above: Originals and a fake: the statues on Schloßbrücke are real, but the false façade behind them was only a temporary measure (right).
below: The flea market next to the ruined Tachele building has a distinct oriental spice to it, like something out of »1001 Arabian Nights«.

Hinter diesen Mauern schaltet und waltet der Regierende Bürgermeister von Berlin: Das Rote Rathaus heißt wegen seiner Fassade so, nicht wegen der politischen Vergangenheit. Davor Reinhold Begas' Neptunbrunnen.

The Mayor of Berlin administrates and controls within these walls. The Red Town Hall is named after its red-brick front, not its political past. Reinhold Begas' Neptune Fountain splashes in front of it.

Applaus: Daß im »Chamäleon« in den Hackeschen Höfen erstklassiges Varieté geboten wird, hat sich sehr schnell herumgesprochen.

Bravo! The word has spread fast that there's first-class entertainment to be had in »Chamäleon« in the Hackesche Höfe.

wirbt. Heine jedenfalls hätte sich bestimmt in die Girlparade dieses Revue-Theaters verguckt. Schließlich schielte er ja schon in seinen »Briefen aus Berlin« nach so mancher »Blondine« und »dahinhüpfenden Nymphe«.

Und von der Friedrichstraße aus würde der per Zeitmaschine ins Heute katapultierte Dichter bestimmt noch einen Abstecher in die morbide Oranienburger machen, wo neuerdings die Bohème zu Hause ist. Sei es in der monströsen Kunstruine des Tacheles, in den Hackeschen Höfen am Südende der Straße oder in einer der vielen Szenekneipen und Gale-

ble, his former place of work. There, new accents are being brought to the Bertolt Brecht and Heiner Müller tradition by the actor Martin Wuttke. As director, his thoughts must be constantly haunted by the Berliner Ensemble's honourable »resident ghosts«. Should the burden of the past become too great, however, he can always pop by his neighbour and competitor, the Deutsches Theater, for a little distraction. Perhaps Wuttke even goes to the new Friedrichstadtpalast to relax, which boasts the 62 most beautiful legs in Berlin. Heine in any case would definitely have been enamoured by this revue theatre's

Kunst, Kultur und Stadt-
geschichte:
**Die Hackeschen Höfe
entwickeln sich zu einem
der lebendigsten Kneipen-
und Kultur-Treffpunkte
der Stadt.**

Art, culture and city
history: the Hackesche
Höfe are rapidly
becoming one of the
city's most lively social
and cultural meeting
places.

rien. Hier läßt sich nachvollziehen, was Franz Biberkopf aus Alfred Döblins Bestseller »Berlin Alexanderplatz« im alten Scheunenviertel erlebt haben mag. Fürs verruchte Feeling sorgen des Nachts die »Bordsteinschwalben«, die unter der frisch vergoldeten Kuppel der Neuen Synagoge auf Kundschaft warten. Ironisch blinken dazu die roten Lichter des Fernsehturms vom Alexanderplatz herüber.

parade of girls, as some of his Letters from Berlin suggest, where he steals glances at blondes and »light-footed nymph[s]«.

If the poet were to be catapulted into the present by time machine, he would most probably take a detour from the Friedrichstraße to the rather degenerate Oranienburger Straße, domicile to the new Bohemia. This is where creative minds hang out in the monstrous artistic ruin of the Tachele, in the Hackesche Höfe at the southern end of the street, or in one of the many pubs or galleries. The atmosphere evokes what Franz Biberkopf in Alfred Döblin's bestseller »Berlin Alexanderplatz« must have experienced in the old Scheunenviertel. At night, the »kerb swallows« radiate an air of disrepute, waiting for customers beneath the freshly gilded dome of the New Synagogue. The red lights of the television tower on Alexanderplatz flash ironically in the background, offering suitable illumination for the more sordid side of the city.

Klassizismus in höchster Vollendung: Durchs Brandenburger Tor dürfen nur Busse, Taxis und Radfahrer fahren. Die Viktoria aus Schadows Quadriga hat ein Auge drauf. Auf dem nahen Reichstag flattert Schwarz, Rot, Gold (oben Mitte).

Classicism to perfection: only buses, taxis and cycles are allowed to drive through the Brandenburg Gate. Victoria in Schadow's »Quadriga« presides over those who pass under her. The black, red and gold of the German flag waves from the nearby Reichstag (top centre).

Von dorischen
Säulen getragen:
Schinkels Neue
Wache dient heute
als zentrale
Gedenkstätte der
Bundesrepublik
Deutschland.
Ganz in der Nähe
gibt der Alte Fritz
die Sporen.

Carried by Doric
pillars: today,
Schinkel's New
Guard House is a
central place of
memorial for the
whole of Germany.
Not far off,
Old Fritz spurs on
his horse.

Die neuen Konsumtempel an der Friedrichstraße. Die Galeries Lafayette nahe dem U-Bahnhof Französische Straße faszinieren im Innern durch einen markanten Glastrichter. Unten rechts das sogenannte Quartier 205.

The new consumer temples on Friedrichstraße. The Galeries Lafayette near the Französische Straße U-Bahn station boast a fascinating glass-funnel interior. »Quartier 205« (such is its nickname) is pictured bottom right.

37

Die Tage des Palasts der Republik nahe der imposanten Dom-Kuppel sind gezählt. Das weiß selbst die Denkmalsfigur des Freiherrn vom Stein (unten).

Unabashedly quadrate next to the round dome of the cathedral, the Palace of the Republic's days are numbered. Freiherr von Stein's imposing statue takes note (bottom).

Obwohl der zu
DDR-Zeiten neuge-
staltete Alexander-
platz nicht gerade
viel Charme ver-
sprüht, läßt sich
dort so mancher
Passant von süd-
amerikanischen
Rhythmen
mitreißen.

Although Alexander-
platz, redesigned
during GDR days,
isn't exactly full of
charm, it doesn't
prevent passers-by
from grooving to
South American
rhythms.

Architektonische Zeugnisse der Stalin-Ära: Am Strausberger Platz beginnt das östliche Gegenstück zum westlichen Kurfürstendamm.

Architectural witnesses to the Stalin era: East Berlin's counterpart to the West sector's Kurfürstendamm starts on Strausberger Platz.

Der Fernsehturm am Alexanderplatz, erbaut zu Zeiten des DDR-Staatsratsvorsitzenden Walter Ulbricht, wird auch »St. Walter« genannt, weil sich auf der Restaurant-Kugel bei Sonnenschein ein Kreuz abzeichnet.

The television tower on Alexanderplatz, built when Walter Ulbricht was GDR's head of state, is also called »St. Walter«, as a cross is lit up by sunlight falling on the restaurant.

Karl Friedrich Schinkel – der Baumeister des Königs

Als einen Visionär mit Charakterkopf stellt uns der Bildhauer Christian Friedrich Tieck seinen Zeitgenossen Karl Friedrich Schinkel (1781–1841) in Marmor vor. In der Hand hält die Denkmalsfigur eine Grundrißskizze – als Verweis auf Schinkels Profession. Zu sehen ist die Skulptur in der von Schinkel entworfenen Friedrichwerderschen Kirche (1830), die als Dependance der Nationalgalerie eine ausführliche Dokumentation über den Meister des Klassizismus zeigt.

Seine Bauten können ganz in der Nähe im Original besichtigt werden: Das Alte Museum am Lustgarten (1830 eröffnet) bildet mit seiner langgestreckten Säulenreihe die städtebauliche Ouvertüre der Museumsinsel; wenige Schritte weiter finden sich die Schloßbrücke (1824) und die bereits 1818 Unter den Linden fertiggestellte Neue Wache. Vor wenigen Jahren paradierte dort noch - gegen alliierte Bestimmungen – die NVA-Ehrenwache, heute dient sie als

Für diesen Bau benutzte Schinkel Fassadenteile eines Danziger Patrizierhauses aus dem 15. Jahrhundert: das Kavaliershaus auf der Pfaueninsel.

Schinkel used parts of a façade from a 15th century patrician house from Gda'nsk for the Kavaliershaus on Peacock Island.

pfleger und Stadtplaner, entwarf mustergültige Bühnenbilder (etwa für Mozarts »Zauberflöte«), malte romantische Landschaften und arbeitete auch als Möbel-Designer. Sein Hauptwerk ist das Schauspielhaus am Gendarmenmarkt, flankiert von Gontards Deutschem und Französischem Dom. Der von Friedrich Wilhelm III. in Auftrag gegebene Theaterbau am »schönsten Platz Berlins« wird heute als Konzerthaus genutzt.

Vom »Erbauer des ewigen Berlin« (»Die Zeit«) stammt zudem das gußeiserne Kriegerdenkmal auf dem Kreuzberg, nicht zu vergessen das Humboldt-Schloß in Tegel und das Schloß Klein-Glienicke.

Direkt vor der Friedrichwerderschen Kirche stand einst die Schinkelsche Bauakedemie (1836), deren Kriegsruine 1962 für das DDR-Außenministerium abgerissen wurde.

Da dieser Bau Ende 1995 seinerseits aus dem Stadtbild getilgt wurde, überlegt man nun, die Bauakademie neu zu errichten. Schinkel, der auf dem Dorotheenstädtischen Friedhof neben vielen prominenten Persönlichkeiten begraben liegt, würde sich darüber bestimmt freuen.

Vom Meister selbst entworfen: Schinkels Grabmonument auf dem Dorotheenstädtischen Friedhof.

Designed by the master himself: Schinkel's tomb in the Dorotheenstadt cemetery.

Der Landschaftsarchitekt

Was Schinkel für die Baukunst, war Peter Josef Lenné (1789 - 1866) als Landschaftsplaner. Der Generaldirektor der königlichen Gärten in Preußen setzte sich mit seinen Potsdamer Parkanlagen ein Denkmal, hat aber auch für Berlin eine enorme Bedeutung, vor allem durch seine Umgestaltung des Tiergartens. Vorbild waren die englischen Landschaftsparks. Sie inspirierten Lenné gleichfalls bei der Pfaueninsel sowie den Schloßparks von Niederschönhausen, Friedrichsfelde (heute Tierpark) und beim

nördlichen Teil des Schloßparks Charlottenburg. Mit Sichtachsen, künstlichen Hügeln und Seen schuf er eine weiträumige Kunstwelt, die mit der Natur im Wettstreit um Schönheit und Harmonie liegt. Ein Gemeinschaftswerk von Schinkel und Lenné sind Schloß und Park von Klein-Glienicke, der Sommerresidenz des Prinzen Karl. Kaum bekannt ist, daß auch der Landwehrkanal auf Lennés Initiative hin gebaut wurde.

Vor Schinkels Altem Museum kämpft die Amazone mit dem Panther.

In front of Schinkel's Old Museum, the amazon battles with a panther.

zentrale Gedenkstätte der Bundesrepublik.

Der in Neuruppin geborene Baumeister kann mit Fug und Recht als Multitalent bezeichnet werden: Schinkel war Architekt, Denkmals-

Karl Friedrich Schinkel – The »Builder of Eternal Berlin«

A visionary with striking features: this is the impression we gain from sculptor Christian Friedrich Tieck's marble statue of his contemporary, Karl Friedrich Schinkel (1781–1841). In his hand, the monumental figure holds a ground plan – a symbol of Schinkel's profession. His statue stands proud in Friedrichwerder Church (1830), which he himself designed, now an annexe of Berlin's National Gallery, where an extensive display on the master of Classicism is accommodated.

Not far from the museum, his buildings can be visited »in the flesh«. The Old Museum in Lustgarten (opened in 1830) forms an urban architectural overture to the museum island with its long row of columns; a few steps further on are his Schloßbrücke (1824) and the New Guard House in Unter den Linden, completed in 1818. Until a few years ago, this was where the honorary guard of the GDR's National People's Army paraded – against Allied stipulations. It now serves as a central memorial for the whole of Germany.

Born in Neuruppin, the master builder can with complete justification be described as multi-talented. Schinkel was an architect, curator of monuments and town planner; he designed exemplary stage sets (for example, for Mozart's »Magic Flute«), painted romantic landscapes and also worked as a designer of furniture.

His main architectural achievement is the Schauspielhaus (theatre) on Gendarmenmarkt, flanked by Gontard's German and French cathedrals. Frederick William III's commissioned theatre building on the »most beautiful square in Berlin« is now used as a concert hall.

The »builder of eternal Berlin« (Die Zeit) also produced the cast-iron war memorial on Kreuzberg, Humbolt's country house, Tegel, and Klein-Glienicke Palace.

Directly in front of Friedrichwerder Church was where Schinkel's Academy of Architecture once stood (1836); its ruins were torn down in 1962 to make way for the GDR's foreign ministry. As the latter building was wiped from the city's panorama at the end of 1995, officials are now considering rebuilding the Academy. Schinkel, buried in the cemetery in Dorotheenstadt alongside many other prominent figures, would probably be most delighted at this proposal.

Durchblick: der Deutsche Dom am Gendarmenmarkt, umrahmt vom antikisierenden Ambiente des Schauspielhauses – Schinkels Hauptwerk.

The German Cathedral on Gendarmenmarkt, framed by the antique ambience of the Schauspielhaus – Schinkel's main architectural achievement.

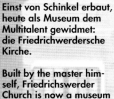

Einst von Schinkel erbaut, heute als Museum dem Multitalent gewidmet: die Friedrichwerdersche Kirche.

Built by the master himself, Friedrichswerder Church is now a museum dedicated to the multi-talented Schinkel.

The Landscape Architect

What Schinkel was to architecture, Peter Josef Lenné (1789 - 1866) was to landscaping. The general director of the royal gardens in Prussia erected a true memorial to himself with his Potsdam parks and was also a figure of great importance for Berlin, especially with his new designs for the Tiergarten Park, which now houses the Berlin Zoo. The many landscaped parks in England were Lenné's models and the inspiration behind his Peacock Island, the parks for Niederschönhausen and Friedrichsfelde Palaces (the latter now a zoo), and the northern area of the park around Charlottenburg Palace. He created an expansive artistic world with artificial hills, lakes, and wonderful views, competing with nature for beauty and harmony. One of Schinkel's and Lenné's joint projects is the Klein-Glienicke palace and park, Prince Carl's summer residence. A little known fact is that the Landwehrkanal was built on Lenné's initiative.

Neu, auf alt getrimmt: Das Niko-laiviertel rund um die Nikolaikirche war 1987 der Bei-trag Ost-Berlins zur 750-Jahrfeier der Stadt. Cafés und Restaurants, aber auch die Original-Fassade des 1935 woanders abgetra-genen Ephraim-Palais (S. 44, oben rechts) sind die Hauptattraktionen.

Something old, something new: the Nikolai Quarter huddled around St. Nicholas' Church was East Berlin's contribution to the 750 Years of Berlin celebration in 1987. Cafés and restau-rants and also the original façade of the Ephraim Palace (p. 44, top right), removed from its original location in 1935, are the main attractions.

Seite 46/47: Lange
Beine, teuflisch
gutes Entertainment
und blitzende Laser:
Bei den großen
Revue-Produktionen
im neuen Friedrich-
stadtpalast wird
nicht an Effekten
gespart.

Page 46/47: Long
legs, flashing lasers
and devilishly good
entertainment: all
the stops are pulled
out for the big revue
special effects in
the new Friedrich-
stadtpalast.

Hier blitzt das
»Rheingold«
musikalisch auf:
Neben der Staats-
oper Unter den
Linden (oben und
unten) sind auch
das Deutsche
Theater mit den
Kammerspielen
(rechts oben) und
das jetzt für
Konzerte reservierte
Schauspielhaus
(rechts Mitte)
der Hochkultur
verpflichtet.

This is where
»Rheingold« fills
Berlin with music:
the Staatsoper in
Unter den Linden
(top and bottom),
the Deutsches
Theater with the
Kammerspiele
(top right) and the
Schauspielhaus
(center right), now
only used for
concerts, are all
dedicated to high
culture.

Rund um die Mitte: im »Hundekopf« der S-Bahn

Round the Centre: the »Canine Head« of the Berlin's City Railway

»Richtung Wartenberg,
bitte einsteigen«:
Gedränge im Bahnhof
Alexanderplatz.
Seite 50: Der eiserne
Kanzler und die goldene
Else: Bismarck im Dialog
mit dem Friedensengel
auf der Siegessäule.

»The train on platform
three is now leaving for
Wartenberg«: hustle and
bustle in Alexanderplatz
Station.
Page 50: The iron chan-
cellor and Golden Else:
Bismarck conversing with
the angel of peace on
Victory Column.

Rrrums! Geräuschvoll schieben sich die Türen per Luftdruck zu, und schon ruckt die S-Bahn mit singendem Ton an. Vom Bahnhof Schöneberg nahe dem Rathaus (vor dem Willy Brandt im November 1989 proklamiert hatte: »Jetzt wächst zusammen, was zusammen gehört«) geht die Fahrt auf dem Südring gen Neukölln. Der Brückenschlag weiter nach Treptow im Osten zählt noch zu den ehrgeizigen Projekten der S-Bahn-Betreiber. Am Nordring liegt gar ein fast zehn Kilometer langer Abschnitt brach. Teilungsbedingt. Erst nach der Jahrtausendwende soll der Schienenstrang in Form eines Hundekopfes

Whoosh! The air-pressured doors close with a swish and the train hums off along its gleaming rails. From Schöneberg Station near the town hall (where Willy Brandt proclaimed in November, 1989: »All that was once one should now reunite«), we travel towards Neukölln on the southern circuit of the S-Bahn, the city rail system. Further towards Treptow in the east of the city, the planned new link is one of the S-Bahn's most ambitious projects. On the northern circuit, a stretch of track almost 10 kilometres long remains disused, the result of urban division. Plans to reopen it are scheduled for the next

Fußbad: Der Tiergarten ist
Berlins Central Park.

Foot bath: Tiergarten is
Berlin's Central Park.

wieder geschlossen sein. Es dauert eben, bis zusammen wächst, was zusammen gehört.

Sobald die Gleise verlegt und die maroden Bahnhöfe renoviert sind, kann die Rundreise in den rot-gelben Waggons auch ohne Unterbrechung beginnen: in 70 Minuten im weiten Bogen um die alte Mitte. Am unteren Ende des Kurfürstendamms schlabbert die Schnauze des S-Bahn-Hundekopfs am Halensee; die Nase schnuppert in den verborgenen Winkeln des barocken Schloßbaus zu Charlottenburg, sofern sie nicht die Witterung im Gebüsch des dazugehörigen Parks aufnimmt; das

Sehen und gesehen werden, flanieren und genießen: Der Kurfürstendamm ist als Boulevard ohne Konkurrenz. Bismarck gab ihn nach dem Vorbild der Champs Elysees in Auftrag.

Seeing and being seen, taking a stroll and enjoying life: this is what the Kurfürstendamm is all about. Bismarck's unique boulevard is modelled on the Champs Elysées in Paris.

Nackenfell sträubt sich am Bahnhof Ostkreuz in Lichtenberg; die Ohren sind an der alternativ bewegten Schönhauser Allee gespitzt; und am Kiefer starten die Regionalflieger auf der Runway des Flughafens Tempelhof.

Dieser Hundekopf umschließt das Kerngebiet des »steinernen Berlin« mit seinen Wohnblöcken und Hinterhöfen, wie sie Werner Hegemann 1930 in seinem Buch über »die größte Mietskasernenstadt der Welt« beschrieben hat. Wichtigste grüne Lunge dieses Molochs aus Ziegeln, Glas und Beton ist der Tiergarten mit dem artenreichsten Zoo, den es gibt,

millennium, finally giving the system back its characteristic dog's head shape. It takes time for things to reunite which were once one.

As soon as the new tracks have been laid and the neglected stations given a fresh lick of paint, our trip in the red-and-yellow carriages can continue without interruption: a wide loop round the old centre of town in 70 minutes. At the bottom end of the Kurfürstendamm, the underground dog's muzzle droops into Halensee Lake; his nose sniffs around in hidden corners of the Baroque Charlottenburg Palace, when not taking in the various scents in the bushes of Charlottenburg's park; the hair on the back of his neck brushes against Ostkreuz Station in Lichtenberg; his ears are tuned in to the alternative scene in Schönhauser Allee; and where his jaw is, regional flights start speeding along the runway of Tempelhof Airport.

This canine head encloses the central area of »stone Berlin« with its blocks of flats and backyards, Werner Hegemann's terminology for the »largest city of tenement houses in the world« in his book from 1930. The most important breath of fresh air in this brick, glass and concrete fortress is offered by Tiergarten Park with the zoo, residence to the largest amal-

Let it groove: Im Jazzclub Quasimodo gibt's kaum noch einen Stehplatz, wenn Größen wie der Saxophonist Wayne Shorter zu Gast sind.

Let it groove: there's hardly room to stand in Quasimodo jazz club when greats like Wayne Shorter make a guest appearance.

Kontrastprogramm:
Wenn Claudio Abbado
einmal nicht im »Zirkus
Karajani« dirigiert, kann
auch Lionel Hampton
beim Jazzfest in der
Philharmonie auftreten.

A programme of con-
trasts: when Claudio
Abbado is not conducting
in »Karajan's Circus«,
Lionel Hampton can take
the stage at the jazz
festival in the
Philharmonic Hall.

und dem Kulturforum, zu dem unter anderem Mies van der Rohes Neue Nationalgalerie, das goldene Bücherschiff der Staatsbibliothek und das philharmonische Pentagon des »Zirkus Karajani« gehören.

Streng genommen führt der S-Bahn-Ring nicht durch die Innenstadt, sondern durch die extrem verdichteten zentralen Bezirke ringsum, die von ihren Dimensionen her alle eigenständige Großstädte sein könnten (und ursprünglich auch waren). Wer also behauptet, das ehemalige West-Berlin sei nichts anderes als ein Agglomerat von Vororten, liegt vollkommen richtig. Selbst der Kurfürstendamm ist eigentlich »nur« die Hauptschlagader von Charlottenburg und Wilmersdorf. Als Boulevard stiehlt »das Schaufenster des Westens« mit seiner Verlängerung, der Tauentzienstraße, bis zum Wittenbergplatz freilich allen andern Berliner Zentren die Schau. Die Geschäftsleute der mondänen Magistrale fürchten weder die Konkurrenz der neuen Kauf-Paläste an der Friedrichstraße, noch sind sie neidisch auf die historischen Linden.

Am »Wasserklops« und rings um den »hohlen Zahn« der Kaiser-Wilhelm-Gedächtniskirche laden Straßencafés und Kinos zu Ruhepausen im quirligen Getriebe ein. Und die beiden

gam of different species in the world There is also the Culture Forum, to which Mies van der Rohe's New National Gallery, the golden book-cum-ship of the State Library and the philharmonic pentagon of »Karajan's Circus« belong.

To be pedantic, the underground circuit doesn't actually go through the centre of town but through the extremely compressed central districts around it, which, judging by their size, could all be independent major cities (which, indeed, they originally were). Whosoever maintains that former West Berlin is nothing but an agglomerate of suburbs is quite correct. Even the Kurfürstendamm or Ku'damm is »nothing more« than Charlottenburg's and Wilmersdorf's aorta. Yet as »the display window of the West«, this boulevard steals the show from all of Berlin's other

Ob bei der Berlinale im
Zoo Palast oder in Frank
Castorfs rebellischer
Volksbühne - kulturell
steppt überall der Bär.

Whether at the Berlinale
in Zoo Palast or in Frank
Castorf's rebel Volks-
bühne, the bear dances
everywhere to the tune of
the arts.

Begegnung der rot-gelben Art: Fast alle S-Bahnen rattern im traditionellen Outfit durch die Stadt und ins Umland. Im Hintergrund die Großbaustelle am Potsdamer Platz.

Strange encounters of the red-and-yellow kind, with the building site on Potsdamer Platz in the background. Nearly all of Berlin's S-Bahn trains rattle through the city and surrounding suburbs in their traditional uniform.

centres, stretching from Tauentzienstraße to Wittenbergplatz. Established and prosperous, the business community of this chic magistral are not the least perturbed by competition from the futuristic shopping centres in the Friedrichstraße, nor are they envious of the historical Unter den Linden.

At the »Wasserklops« globe fountain and around the »hollow tooth« of Emperor William II's Memorial Church, street cafés and cinemas entice passers-by to take a break from the frantic hustle and bustle. The two Ku'damm institutions Kranzler and Möhring both try (at least in a culinary sense) to recreate the tradition of the Romanisches Café, a meeting point where the avant-garde of the Golden Twenties came together, from the dramatist Ernst Toller to the Dadaist George Grosz, who caricatured Berlin's demimonde so inimitably. Today, in place of the Romanisches Café, the 22-storey Europa-Center towers towards the heavens. On its roof, Mercedes Benz's advertising-effective star gently rotates around its axis. The infamous Bahnhof Zoo, visible from here and now heavily refurbished, does not belong to the dog's head circuit, but makes up part of the diagonal tram and rail system.

People have been lamenting for years over the decline of the Ku'damm to nothing more than a messy avenue of fast-food joints, yet it is still the place to go for a gentle stroll, to see and be seen. Galleries, bistros and boutiques flourish in the side-streets, all slightly more expensive than anywhere else, but the more tasteful for it. The cultural highlight of this promenade mile is the theatre with its variety of performing arts; there are also comedies

Die Marienkirche in Mitte, eines der ältesten Gotteshäuser Berlins, wird scheinbar von Kreuzberger Wohnmaschinen erdrückt.

St. Mary's Church in the Mitte district, one of Berlin's oldest places of worship, seems crushed by Kreuzberg's high-rise monsters.

Ku'damm-Institutionen Kranzler und Möhring versuchen (zumindest kulinarisch), an die Tradition des Romanischen Cafés anzuknüpfen, jenem Künstlertreff, in dem sich die Avantgarde der Goldenen Zwanziger ihr Stelldichein gab: vom Dramatiker Ernst Toller bis zum Dadaisten George Grosz, der die Berliner Halbwelt so unnachahmlich karikierte. Anstelle des Romanischen Cafés ragt heute das 22stöckige Europa Center in die Luft. Auf dessen Dach zieht der werbewirksame Stern aus Stuttgart-Untertürkheim gemächlich seine Kreise. Der inzwischen aufgemöbelte Bahnhof Zoo in Sichtweite gehört nicht zum Hundekopf, sondern ist Teil der Stadtbahn-Diagonale.

Über den Niedergang des Kurfürstendamms zum Fastfood- und Schmuddel-Boulevard wird zwar seit Jahren lamentiert, trotzdem trifft man sich hier nach wie vor zum Bummeln, Sehen und Gesehenwerden. In den Seitenstraßen florieren Galerien, Bistros und Boutiquen, alle ein bißchen teurer als anderswo, dafür aber auch geschmackvoller. Kulturell bietet die Flaniermeile mit der Schaubühne ein Highlight der darstellenden Künste, Komödie und Theater am Kurfürstendamm halten boulevardesk dagegen. Nach den Vorstellungen muß Madame auf Monsieur aufpassen, denn sobald es dunkel wird, locken die Asphaltsirenen zu sündigem Treiben. Auch das gehört zur Tradition des Ku'damms.

Angelegt wurde der Boulevard anstelle des früheren königlichen Reitweges zum Jagdschloß Grunewald. Die Pariser Champs Elysées vor Augen, erließ Bismarck eine Kabinettsordre, nach der die Prachtstraße 53 Meter breit sein sollte, mit einem Reitweg in der Mitte, der längst von parkenden PS-Kutschen in Beschlag genommen wurde.

Gleichzeitig mit dem Ku'damm entstand südlich des Halensees die Villenkolonie Grunewald, jenes »Millionärskaff«, wie der Kritiker Alfred Kerr spöttelte, obwohl er sich selbst in dieser Gegend niederließ. Wie so viele mußte er nach der Machtergreifung der Nazis emigrieren. So blieb ihm das schlimme Schicksal seiner jüdischen Nachbarn erspart, deren Weg von der sogenannten »Rampe« am Bahnhof Grunewald geradewegs in die Vernichtungslager führte...

Bei der High-Society von heute sind die Grunewalder Filetgrundstücke

Schicke Büros mit noblem Hotel: die Neubauten am Moabiter Spreebogen.

Fancy offices and a posh hotel: new buildings on the Moabit bend of the River Spree.

and more lowbrow shows which help maintain the Ku'damm's boulevard character. After the show, however, Madame had better keep an eye on Monsieur, for as soon as the street lamps begin to flicker, the ladies of the night will entice him to partake in other pastimes, also part and parcel of Ku'damm tradition.

The boulevard was laid out in place of the royal bridleway leading to Grunewald hunting lodge. With the Parisian Champs Elysées in mind, Bismarck issued an order that his new magnificent avenue should be 53 metres wide with a bridleway running down the centre; the latter has long since been commandeered by parked motorised coaches.

South of the Halensee, the Grunewald villa quarter sprang up at the same time as the Ku'damm, and was mockingly referred to by critic Alfred

Und der Haifisch, der hat Zähne: Im Zoo-Aquarium schwimmt, krabbelt, kraucht und schlängelt allerlei Getier. Darunter das Elefantentor zum Zoo.

All sorts of creatures swim, crawl, slide and slither around in the Zoo's aquarium. Below, the Elephant Gate of the Zoo.

trotzdem noch genauso beliebt wie bei den Oberen Zehntausend von damals. Dort wohnen VIPs wie der Filmproduzent Artur Brauner oder die Nachfahren des letzten deutschen Kaisers. Neu hinzugezogen sind im Hauptstadtsog so manche Botschafter und Bankiers. Repräsentation muß sein.

Was für den Adel von Geld oder Geburt recht sein mag, das sollte für die hochgeschätzte Arbeiterklasse im Ost-Berliner Bezirk Friedrichshain der III. SED-Parteitag bewerkstelligen. Nach dessen Beschluß wurde in den fünfziger Jahren die Stalin-Allee (heute Karl-Marx-Allee) als 80 Meter breiter »Boulevard der Werktätigen« angelegt, ein ideologischer Gegenentwurf zum Kurfürstendamm. 45.000 Ost-Berliner begannen zunächst mit der Enttrümmerung, um dann rechts und links der Straße 2000 Wohnun-

Kerr as the »millionaire's dump«, although he lived there himself. Like so many, he was forced to emigrate after the Nazis came to power. He was thus spared the dreadful fate of his Jewish neighbours, whose journey from the »ramp« at Grunewald Station lead straight to the concentration camps.

Despite this, Grunewald's golden estate is as much favoured by today's high-society as it was by the top ten thousand of yesterday. This is VIP territory, where film producers such as Artur Brauner live, or the descendants of the last German emperor. New residents of the capital's showpiece include ambassadors and bank managers. One must retain one's image.

Whereas property is bestowed upon the aristocracy by wealth and birthright, the highly-esteemed working

Und hier spielt die Musik: Philharmonie und Kammermusiksaal, architektonische Meisterwerke von Hans Scharoun.

Strike up the band: the Philharmonic Hall and the Hall of Chamber Music, architectural masterpieces by Hans Scharoun.

Gründerzeit und Postmoderne: das Theater des Westens neben dem Kant-Dreieck mit dem Windsegel.

Gründerzeit and postmodernism: the Theater des Westens next to the Kant Triangle with its giant weathercock sail.

Klarheit und Transparenz sind die Leitgedanken von Mies van der Rohes Neuer Nationalgalerie am Kulturforum.

Shining through: St. Matthew's Church between Alexander Calder's steel sculpture »Têtes et Queue« and Mies van der Rohe's New National Gallery.

gen hochzuziehen, alle mit Bädern und Parkettböden. Als größtes Baudenkmal Berlins werden die Blöcke nach und nach auf Vordermann gebracht, die dafür nötigen Millionen fließen aus diversen Immobilienfonds.

Während dieses Geschäft brummt, klagen die Ladeninhaber an der Karl-Marx-Allee über ausbleibende Kundschaft. Die Leute tauschen ihr Kapital lieber weiter östlich in Waren und Dienstleistungen um: beiderseits des Bahnhofs Frankfurter Allee. Und da sind wir auch schon wieder am S-Bahn-Hundekopf. An der hinteren Schädelplatte.

class in the Friedrichshain district of East Berlin were granted this by the third SED party conference. Following a decree, it built the Stalin-Allee (now the Karl-Marx-Allee) in the Fifties, an 80-metre wide »boulevard of the working people«, the ideological mirror-image of the Ku'damm. 45,000 East Berlin residents began clearing away the rubble from the Second World War and then built 2,000 flats on both sides of the street, all of them with bathrooms and parquet floors. As Berlin's greatest architectural monument, these blocks are now gradually being restored, with the necessary millions of German marks being pumped into the project from various real estate funds.

With all this going on, the shopkeepers on the Karl-Marx-Allee complain of lack of business. People much prefer to exchange their capital for goods and services further east, namely around Frankfurter Allee Station. And by pure coincidence we find ourselves back on our dog's head circuit. At the back of his skull.

Bei der Love-Parade treffen sich einmal pro Jahr Hunderttausende von »Ravern« in schriller Aufmachung und verwandeln die Straße des 17. Juni in die größte Open-air-Disco der Welt.

Hundreds of thousands of ravers in glaring colour meet at the Love Parade every year and turn the Straße des 17. Juni into the biggest open-air disco in the world.

Seite 58/59:
Die Siegessäule –
martialische Erinne-
rung an preußische
Kriege, heute heim-
liches Wahrzeichen
der Schwulenszene
Berlins.

Page 58/59:
The Victory Column
– a martial reminder
of Prussian wars,
but also the secret
symbol of Berlin's
gay scene.

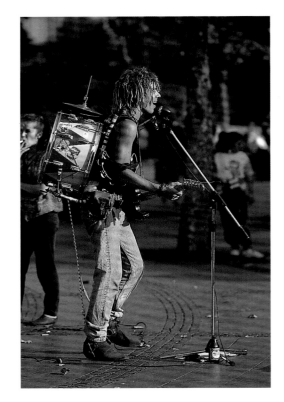

60

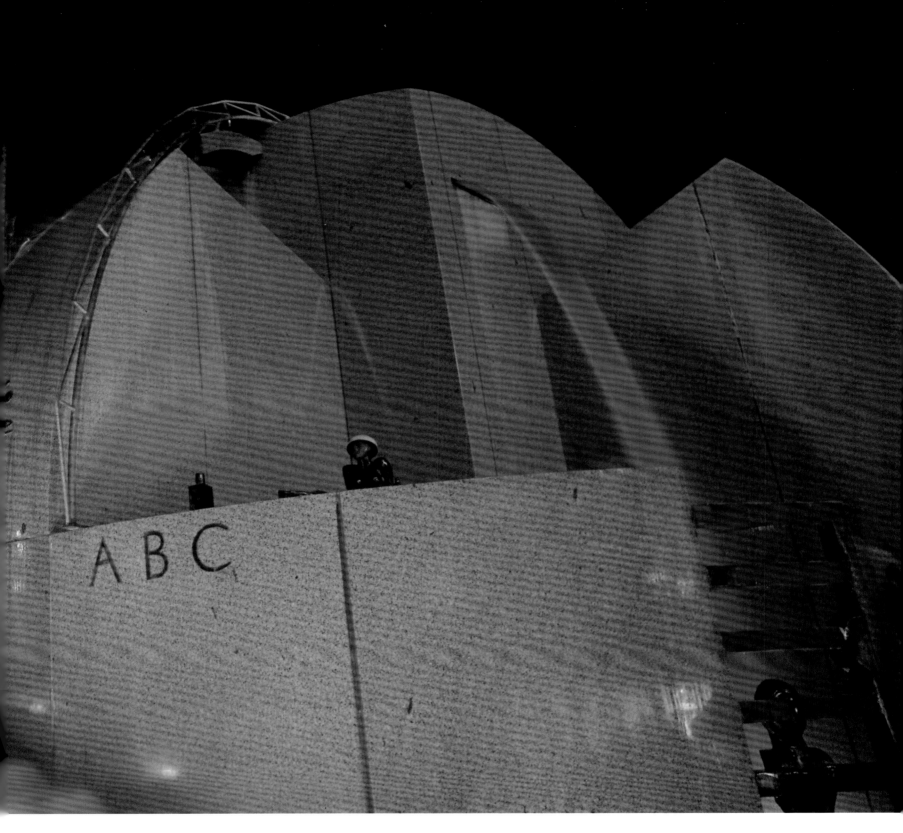

Seite 60/61: High-
life rund um
Joachim Schmettaus
Weltkugel-Brunnen.
Flankiert wird der
»Wasserklops« vom
Europa Center und
der Kaiser-Wilhelm-
Gedächtniskirche.

Page 60/61: Highl-
ife around Joachim
Schmettau's globe
fountain. The »Was-
serklops« is flanked
by the Europa-
Center and Emperor
William II's Memo-
rial Church.

Oben: Umschlungen von den stählernen »Maxi-Makkaronis« des Künstlerpaars Brigitte und Martin Matschinsky-Denninghoff: die Kaiser-Wilhelm-Gedächtniskirche. Unten und rechts: Aber bitte mit Sahne: »konditern jehn« am Kurfürstendamm, zum Beispiel in den Institutionen Möhring und Kranzler.

Top: Entwined by artist couple Brigitte and Martin Matschinsky-Denninghoff's steel »maxi-macaroni«: Emperor William II's Memorial Church. Bottom and to the right: Don't forget the cream: eating cake on Kurfürstendamm in institutions such as Möhring and Kranzler.

»Langer Lulatsch«:
der Funkturm auf
dem Messegelände,
erbaut für die Funk-
ausstellung 1926.
Drei Jahre später
wurde von ihm das
allererste Fernseh-
bild ausgestrahlt.

»Long beanpole«:
the radio tower in
the grounds of the
exhibition centre
was built for the
radio exhibition in
1926. Three years
later, it transmitted
the first television
pictures.

Mietet sich hier ein
Ministerium ein?
Gläserne Gletscher-
zungen im Moabiter
Spreebogen.
Das Internationale
Congress Centrum
hat sogar einen
eigenen Auto-
bahnanschluß und
ein Postamt.

Is a ministry going
to take these lod-
gings or not? Glassy
glacial walls on the
Moabit bend of the
River Spree.
The International
Congress Centre
has even got its
own motorway exit
and a post office.

Seite 66/67:
Abschalten und
relaxen im Herzen
der Millionen-
Metropole. In einer
Niesche des Land-
wehrkanals
(rechts unten)
können sogar ein
paar Hausboote vor
sich hindümpeln.

Page 66/67:
Switching off and
relaxing in the heart
of the giant metro-
polis. On a quiet
stretch of the Land-
wehrkanal (bottom
right) there's even
room for a few
house-boats to bob
up and down.

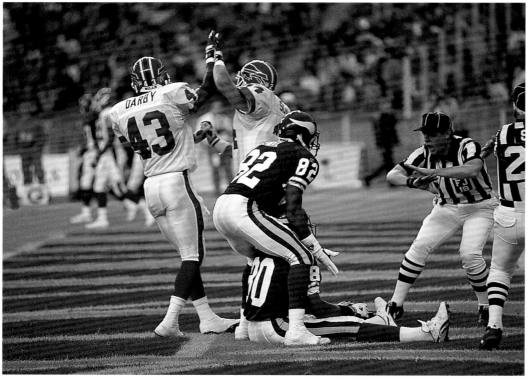

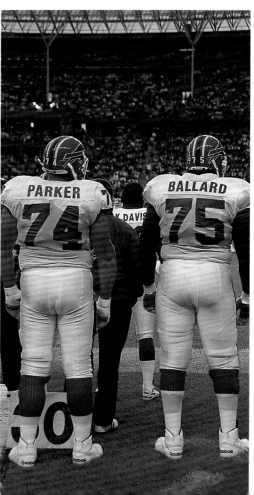

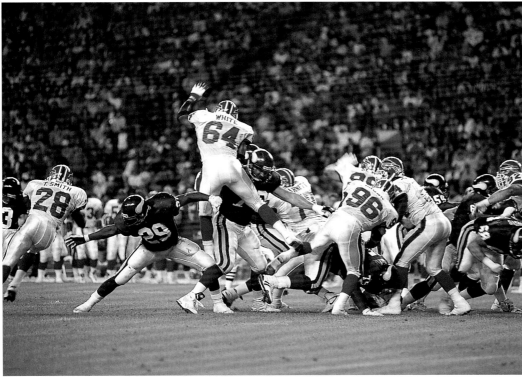

Vom Pas de deux im Wartestand zum Corps de ballet der Kampfmaschinen. Ausverkauft: Ob beim Länderspiel, beim Papstbesuch oder wie hier beim American Football – 76.000 Zuschauer bilden in Werner Marchs Olympiastadion von 1936 immer wieder eine imposante Kulisse.

From a pas de deux while waiting to a corps de ballet of fighting machines. Sold out: whether for an international match, a visit from the Pope or American football, the 76,000 spectators in Werner March's Olympic Stadium from 1936 always form an impressive backdrop.

Repräsentation muß sein: Schloß und Park von Charlottenburg bilden ein harmonisches Gesamtkunstwerk. Der verschneite Weg führt zum Mausoleum der 1810 gestorbenen Königin Luise. Friedrich Wilhelm III. überlebte seine Frau um 30 Jahre und wurde dann an der Seite der populären Monarchin beigesetzt – wie sie in einem Sarkophag von Christian Daniel Rauch.

Representing the city: Charlottenburg Palace and Gardens form a harmonious artistic unit. The snowy path leads to Queen Luise's mausoleum. The queen died in 1810; her husband, Frederick William III, survived her by 30 years and now lies buried alongside the popular monarch. Both rest in sarcophagi made by Christian Daniel Rauch.

Seite 72: Die neu-
gotische Oberbaum-
brücke verbindet
die Bezirke
Kreuzberg und
Friedrichshain.
Zu Mauerzeiten war
sie ein Nadelöhr
für Wessis und Ossi-
Rentner.

Page 72: Kreuzberg
and Friedrichshain
are joined by the
neo-Gothic Ober-
baum Bridge. While
the Wall still stood,
it was the eye of a
needle for »Wessis«
(West Germans) and
pensioners from the
East.

Kiezidyllen finden
sich im legeren
Straßencafé
genauso wie am
Prenzelberger
Wassertum oder
im Friseurmuseum
an der Husemann-
straße.

Urban idyll radiates
from street cafés,
the water tower in
Prenzelberg or the
Hairdressing
Museum in
Husemannstraße.

ZU BESUCH
BEI DEN »BERGVÖLKERN«

Nein, in Kreuzberg braucht's keinen Bodyguard, um unbehelligt zu einer der vielen Szenekneipen an der Oranienstraße oder der Hasenheide zu gelangen. Das gleiche gilt für Schöneberg und den Bezirk Prenzlauer Berg, Deutschlands größtes Altbau-Sanierungsgebiet und zugleich Lieblingsrevier der alternativen Nachtschwärmer. Bei den Berliner »Bergvölkern« mag's zwar schrill und

Nachmittags tauscht man am Prenzelberg das Wohnzimmer gern mit dem Straßencafé.

Afternoon: swopping your living room for one of the street cafés in Prenzelberg.

unkonventionell zugehen, die Klischees vom heißen Pflaster sind aber meist an den Haaren herbeigezogen.

In SO 36 – so heißt die »bewegte« nördliche Hälfte Kreuzbergs nach einem alten Postzustellbezirk – bilden Punks, Gastarbeiterfamilien aus Anatolien, Studenten, Künstler und Berliner »Ureinwohner« eine quirlige Melange. Wenn der Dampfkessel mal wieder überkocht, steht das zwar in dicken Lettern in den Gazetten, ansonsten lebt sich's dennoch ganz beschaulich im Kiez.

Die Kreuzberger Nächte sind natürlich immer noch so lang wie zu Zeiten der Gebrüder Blattschuß, die den entsprechend betitelten Kneipen-Hymnus zum Ohrwurm gemacht

haben. Da es in Berlin keine Sperrstunde gibt, kann in den von Fall zu Fall wechselnden In-Schuppen bis zum frühen Morgen durchgemacht werden. Die Raver halten es in ihren Techno-Tempeln sogar bis zum Mittag des folgenden Tages aus. Dafür geht in den gerade »angesagten« Läden die Post auch erst nach zwei Uhr nachts so richtig ab.

Entwickeln konnte sich die Kreuzberger Szene, weil die Loft-Mieten für Wohngemeinschaften in den siebziger und achtziger Jahren noch sehr niedrig lagen. Aus dem gleichen Grund wächst jetzt die Prenzelberger Bohème mehr und mehr. Kulturbrauerei und Pfefferberg heißen hier die Zentren der Off-Kultur, beide an der Schönhauser Allee.

Die Tresen-Trotter finden sich dafür beim »Zug um die Häuser« meistens rund um den Kollwitzplatz oder den (von mehreren Mietparteien bewohnten) Wasserturm nahe der Rykestraße wieder. Und sei es auch nur zum Talk über die letzte Premiere an der Volksbühne, genannt »Panzerkreuzer vom Prenzlauer Berg«. Dabei liegt Frank Castorfs rebellisches Theater gerade noch in Mitte. Aber was macht das schon? Kreuz- und Prenzelberg sind eine Frage des Lebensgefühls, nicht der Geographie, zumal auch große Teile von Mitte zur Szene gehören – abseits der Regierungsbauten, des Gendarmenmarkts und der Pracht Unter den Linden.

Kleinkunst und Comedy: Die »singende Tellermiene« Palma Kunkel hat ihren Kollegen Detlef Winterberg zum Grünen Mittwochssalon an den Rosa-Luxemburg-Platz geladen.

Comedy and cabaret: »singing plate-face« Palma Kunkel has invited her colleague Detlef Winterberg to the Green Wednesday Salon on Rosa-Luxemburg-Platz.

VISITING BERLIN'S »HILL PEOPLE«

No, you don't need a bodyguard in Kreuzberg to get to one of the many bars and pubs in the Oranienstraße or Hasenheide. Nor do you need a sturdy companion in Schöneberg or the Prenzlauer Berg district, Germany's largest housing redevelopment area and favourite territory for alternative night owls. Berlin's »hill people« may be loud and unconventional, but clichés of their patch being a dangerous one are rather far-fetched.

In SO 36 – Kreuzberg's »turbulent« northern half is named after an old postcode – punks, families of Anatolian immigrant workers, students, artists and »original« Berlin residents make up an effervescent melange. Local and national rags naturally report any instances of this strange mixture boiling over in big, thick letters, but mostly life is quiet. Kreuzberg nights are still as long as proclaimed by the Blattschuß brothers in their catchy old pub favourite. As there are no official closing times in Berlin, you can party on into the early hours wherever it's all happening. Ravers even manage to keep going until midday the next day in their techno temples, although the fun doesn't start in the designated joint until about two in the morning. The development of the Kreuzberg scene was heavily assisted by low rents for people sharing flats in converted factory units in the Seventies and Eighties. The Prenzelberg Bohemia is thus now expanding at a terrific rate. The off-culture centres of the area are the Kulturbrauerei and Pfefferberg, both in the Schönhauser Allee.

Bar hoppers mostly meet up with each other again after their »crawl round the houses« on Kollwitzplatz or at the water tower (inhabited by several groups of tenants) near Rykestraße. They may only just want to discuss the latest premiere at the Volksbühne, affectionately called the »Prenzlauer Berg armoured cruiser«, whereby Frank Castorf's rebel theatre is actually in the Mitte district. But what does that matter? Kreuzberg and Prenzelberg are a question of sense of living, not geography, especially as much of the Mitte

district is also part of the scene – a far cry from the government buildings, the Gendarmenmarkt and the splendour of Unter den Linden.

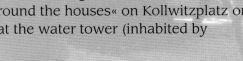

Ungewöhnliche Begegnung der künstlerischen Art: Berliner Hinterhöfe wie dieser an der Oranienburger Straße sind immer gut für eine Entdeckungstour.

Strange encounters of the artistic kind: Berlin's backyards, such as this one in Oranienburger Straße, are always rewarding on tours of discovery.

Bechern auf schwankenden Planken: Auf der Van Loon im Kreuzberger Urban-Hafen gehen die Zecher aus dem Kiez vor Anker.

Drinking on floating boards: local boozers dropping anchor aboard the Van Loon in the Kreuzberg Urban Harbour.

Kiez-Kultur: Vor dem Zosch in der Tucholskystraße sucht ein Filmteam die richtige Einstellung, die die Hinterhofgaleristen längst gefunden haben.

Unten links: Den wuchtigen Hochbunker an der Reinhardtstraße haben Techno- und Lederfans in Beschlag genommen.

Seite 77: Blütenträume auf dem Trabi: Die »Rennpappe« ist eine aussterbende Spezies, um die sich schon zahlreiche Fanclubs kümmern.

Local culture: a film team setting up in front of the Zosch in Tucholskystraße. Backyard gallery owners have long since found their particular setting.

Bottom left: Techno and leather fans have seized the massive stronghold in Reinhardtstraße.

Page 77: Floral dreams on a Trabant. The »cardboard racer« is slowly dying out, yet has a huge following in the form of numerous fan clubs.

Brandmauer-
Ästhetik mit Hirn
am Kreuzberger
Thomas Thomas-Weiß-
becker-Haus in der
südlichen Wilhelm-
straße.

Fire-wall aesthetics
with brains on the
side of the Thomas
Weißbecker House
in Kreuzberg, south
Wilhelmstraße.

Kreuzberger Kon-
traste: traditioneller
Gründerzeit-Stuck
am Planufer und
türkisches Leben in
der Skalitzer- und
Oranienstraße.

Kreuzberg con-
trasts: traditional
Gründerzeit archi-
tecture on Planufer
and Turkish life in
Skalitzerstraße and
Oranienstraße.

Oben: Neogotisch: Das Schinkel-Denkmal auf dem Kreuzberg (Viktoriapark) erinnert an die Freiheitskriege gegen Napoléon und gilt als Wahrzeichen des Bezirks.

Unten und rechts: Für große Kunst- und Ausstellungsspektakel reserviert: der Martin-Gropius-Bau an der Stresemannstraße.

Seite 82/83: Paare, Passanten: Laisserfaire vor bröckelnden Altbau-Fassaden.

Top: Neo-Gothic: the Schinkel Monument on Kreuzberg Hill (Victoria Park) commemorates the Wars of Liberation against Napoleon and is the district's symbol.

Bottom and right: Reserved for major exhibitions: the Martin Gropius Building in Stresemannstraße.

Page 82/83: Couples and passers-by: laisser-faire in front of the crumbling façades of old buildings.

Köpenick, Spandau, Zehlendorf – die Aussenbezirke

Köpenick, Spandau, Zehlendorf – the Outlying Districts

Der Schein trügt: Nicht etwa im Spreewald, sondern in Neu-Venedig, einem Ortsteil von Köpenick, findet sich diese Idylle.

Appearances are deceptive: this idyllic setting is not in the Spreewald, but in »New Venice«, part of Köpenick.

Seite 84: Ganz schön barock: die Köpenicker Schloßkapelle nach Plänen von Johann Arnold Nering.

Page 84: Very Baroque: the Köpenick Palace Chapel, designed by Johann Arnold Nering.

Die drei Wälzer des Berliner Telefonbuchs sind doch immer wieder ein Born der Freude. Wehe, wer etwa auf den 31 Müller-Seiten den richtigen Anschluß sucht. Selbst bei den Voigts steht vor der Wahl die Qual der Nummernsuche: auf vier Seiten im Band von R bis Z. Wilhelm Voigt ist da mit seinen fünf Namensvettern noch ein vergleichsweise einfacher Fall. In Köpenick wohnt allerdings keiner von ihnen. Dabei würde ein Träger dieses Namens so gut in den grünen Außenbezirk passen, war es doch der mittellose Schuster Wilhelm Voigt, der Köpenick weltweit bekannt gemacht hatte: durch ein Bubenstück, über das

The three heavy tomes of Berlin's telephone directory are always a bundle of fun. Good luck to the poor person who's looking for the right number on 31 pages of Müllers. Even with the Voigts you're not much better off: they take up 4 pages from R to Z. Compared to this, Wilhelm Voigt with a mere five contemporaries of the same name is a relatively simple case. Yet none of them live in Köpenick, which is a shame, as the bearer of this name would fit so well in the green outlying district. For it was a Wilhelm Voigt, an impoverished cobbler, who put Köpenick firmly on the world map in 1906 with

Naherholung: Der
Schlachtensee im Grune-
wald läßt schnell den
nahen Millionen-Moloch
vergessen.
Unten: Der Grunewald-
turm bietet eine prächtige
Aussicht über die weit-
läufige Wald- und Havel-
landschaft.

Relaxation: city stress
soon melts away at the
Schlachtensee in Grune-
wald.
Bottom: Grunewald
Tower offers magnificent
views of the expansive
areas of forest and
countryside along the
Havel River.

1906 selbst Majestät schmunzeln mußte.

Mit einer Uniform vom Kostümverleih machte der Schuster das preußische Prinzip von Befehl und Gehorsam lächerlich. Obendrein klaute er noch die Kasse aus dem gerade erbauten neugotischen Rathaus. Carl Zuckmayer hat den gewitzten Kerl mit dem 1931 uraufgeführten »Hauptmann von Köpenick« unsterblich gemacht.

Der Müggelsee, dazu die Köpenicker Wälder ringsum oder das barocke Insel-Schloß - all das stiftet in dem südöstlichen Stadtteil bei weitem kein so großes Identitätsgefühl wie der falsche Hauptmann. Dabei ging es Wilhelm Voigt doch bloß um ein bißchen Anerkennung und ein paar Moneten.

Westliche Schwester des östlichen Köpenick ist Spandau, ursprünglich ebenfalls eine Fischersiedlung. Das Wort vom (gut nachbarschaftlichen) Kiez hat hier wie dort seinen Ursprung. Als waschechte Berliner sehen sich weder die Köpenicker noch die Spandauer, dafür pflegt man einen ausgeprägten Lokalpatriotismus im Nahbereich. Wenn die Spandauer »Separatisten« über eine ihrer sieben Havelbrücken ostwärts fahren, dann sind sie ihrem Selbstverständnis nach unterwegs nach Berlin.

a knavish trick that even brought a smile to royal lips.

The cobbler made a farce of the Prussian principle of order and obedience with a uniform borrowed from a costume agency. On top of this, he also stole the cashbox from the newly-built Neo-Gothic town hall. Carl Zuckmayer's cunning character became immortal with the premiere of his play »The Captain of Köpenick« in 1931.

Müggelsee Lake with the surrounding Köpenick forest, or the Baroque Palace Island - neither bestow such a great sense of identity upon this suburb in the south-east of the city as the false captain. And all because Wilhelm Voigt was hankering after a bit of recognition and some ready cash.

Köpenick's sister and good neighbour in the west is Spandau, originally also a fishing community. Neither the residents of Köpenick nor of Spandau consider themselves to be genuine Berliners, and both nurture a strong feeling of local patriotism. Only when the Spandau »separatists« cross one of their seven bridges over the Havel River do they consider themselves to be in Berlin.

Not only Wilhelm Voigt had moneytroubles. During the emperor's reign, the people from Spandau constantly had to be on the alert against possible procurers of the Reich's »war treasures«, (jokers like the cobbler Voigt, perhaps), stashed away in the Julius Tower of Spandau's Citadel. 1,200 chests each containing 100,000 gold marks were kept in this German Fort Knox, built at the end of the 16th century in the style of an Italian fortress. The Julius Tower even goes back to the beginning of the 14th century. Its massive armoured door today still

Berlin		Tag / Day	Nacht / Night
Temperaturen	Januar	1,7° C	– 3,5° C
	Februar	2,9° C	– 3,1° C
	März	7,8° C	– 0,3° C
	April	13,5° C	3,8° C
	Mai	19,1° C	7,9° C
	Juni	22,3° C	11,1° C
	Juli	23,8° C	13,3° C
	August	23,3° C	12,6° C
	September	19,5° C	9,3° C
	Oktober	13,0° C	5,3° C
	November	6,9° C	1,9° C
	Dezember	3,1° C	– 1,4° C

Seine liebe Not mit dem lieben Geld hatte freilich nicht nur Wilhelm Voigt. Auch die Spandauer mußten zur Kaiserzeit ganz schön auf dem Quivive sein, denn sonst hätte womöglich jemand den »Reichskriegsgoldschatz« aus dem Juliusturm der Spandauer Zitadelle requiriert, trickreich wie der Schuster Voigt. 1200 Kisten mit jeweils 100.000 Goldmark lagerten seinerzeit in diesem »Fort Knox«, das Ende des 16. Jahrhunderts nach dem Vorbild italienischer Festungsbauten errichtet wurde. Der Juliusturm datiert sogar vom Anfang des 14. Jahrhunderts. Seine massige Panzertür zeugt noch heute vom einst so gut be-

bears witness to the once heavily-guarded state treasure.

Money is also a major trait of Zehlendorf. Yet here one doesn't speak about it - one simply has it. At least one has if one resides in one of the palatial villas near the Wannsee or in elegant Dahlem. The latter is often called »Little Oxford« due to its large number of research institutes. It is a first-class address for scientists and the place where Albert Einstein also carried out some of his research. In the Thirties, Otto Hahn, Lise Meitner and Fritz Straßmann discovered nuclear fission here. They could only vaguely imagine the consequences

James Bond 007 läßt grüßen: Die Glienicker Brücke zwischen Potsdam und Berlin war zu DDR-Zeiten Ort spektakulärer Agenten-Austausch-Aktionen.

Like something out of a James Bond film: Glienicke Bridge between Potsdam and Berlin was where spectacular exchanges of secret agents took place between East and West.

hüteten Staatsschatz.

Auch in Zehlendorf ist das Geld das große Thema. Allerdings spricht man nicht davon - man hat es ganz einfach. Zumindest, wenn man in einer der hochherrschaftlichen Villen nahe des Wannsees oder im feinen Dahlem residiert. Letzteres wird wegen der zahlreichen Institute gern »Klein-Oxford« genannt. Ein Wissenschaftsstandort erster Güte, an dem auch Albert Einstein forschte. Otto Hahn entdeckte hier zusammen mit Lise Meitner und Fritz Straßmann in den dreißiger Jahren die Kernspaltung. Die Konsequenzen konnten sie nur vage vorausahnen. Doch schon 1945 gab der damalige amerikanische Präsident Harry S. Truman im Rahmen der Potsdamer Konferenz den Befehl für den Abwurf der ersten Atombombe über dem japanischen Hiroshima. Ort des Geschehens war das »Weiße Haus« am Griebnitzsee, der direkt an Zehlendorf grenzt. Bis 1989 schipperten auf ihm die DDR-Grenztruppen in Militärbooten.

Zehlendorf wird noch von anderen Gegensätzen bestimmt. Da tummeln sich einerseits am Strandbad Tausende in den grünlichen Fluten, frei nach dem Conny-Froboess-Ohrwurm »Pack die Badehose ein, nimm dein kleines Schwesterlein, und dann nischt wie raus nach Wannsee«. Am Ufer gegenüber erinnert andererseits eine Villa an die verhängnisvolle Wannsee-Konferenz, bei der 1942 die sogenannte »Endlösung der Judenfrage« ausgehandelt wurde.

Pfaueninsel, Schloß Klein-Glienicke und das Blockhaus Nikolskoe atmen wiederum den Geist von Preußens Arkadien. Verbindendes Element zu den Schlössern jenseits der Stadtgrenze in Potsdam ist die Glienicker Brücke, zu DDR-Zeiten sinnigerweise

Aber am Wochenende ist's knüppeldicke voll: die Havelchaussee im Grunewald.

The Havelchaussee in Grunewald is always absolutely packed at the weekends.

this would have. Yet only a decade or so later, at the Potsdam summit in 1945, the then American president, Harry S. Truman, gave the order to drop the first atom bomb on Hiroshima. The »scene of the crime« was the »White House« on the Griebnitzsee, bordering on Zehlendorf. Up until 1989, the most frequent patrons of the lake were GDR border guards in their military boots.

Zehlendorf is characterised by very different things. On one side of the lake, thousands romp around on the beach and in the green waters, just like in the popular song by Conny Froboess: »Pack your swimsuit and grab your little sister - we're off to the Wannsee«. Yet a villa on the other side of the lake sternly reminds us of the fateful Wannsee Conference, where in 1942 the so-called »final solution to the Jewish problem« was deliberated.

In pleasant contrast, Peacock Island, Klein-Glienicke Palace and the Nikolskoe log cabin breathe the spirit of Prussia's Arcadia. The palaces beyond the city boundary in Potsdam are linked to the old west sector by the Glienicke Bridge, ironically referred to as »Unity Bridge« in the GDR era. This was where spectacular exchanges of secret agents took place. Schäferberg Hill bulges up over

Auch Fischers Fritz fischt frische Fische im Tegeler Fließ.

Fisherman Fritz also fishes fresh fish in Tegel River.

»Brücke der Einheit« genannt. Sie war Ort spektakulärer Agenten-Austausch-Aktionen. Über allem wölbt sich der Schäferberg, obendrauf ein Fernmeldeturm, den bestimmt schon alle Müllers aus dem Berliner Telefonbuch genutzt haben, um mit Posemuckel oder dem Rest der Welt zu plaudern.

the whole ensemble, the telecommunications tower perched on top of it, probably used at one time or another by all the Müllers in Berlin's telephone directory, trying to ring their sweethearts or the rest of the world for a chat.

Menschen am Sonntag oder »Eine Landpartie« am Stadtrand.

Sunday People or A Country Outing on the Edge of Town.

Seite 90/91: Die preußische Geschichte hat Licht- und Schatten- seiten. Im Schinkel- Schloß Klein- Glienicke, in Sicht- weite Potsdams, erstrahlt sie aber voller Anmut und Würde.

Page 90/91: Prus- sian history has its dark sides. Yet here it emanates grace and dignity in Schinkel's Klein- Glienicke Palace, visible from Potsdam.

»...und dann nischt wie raus nach Wannsee«: Die Eiszeit hat das populäre Freizeitrevier im Südwesten geformt.

»We're off to the Wannsee!« The popular leisure area to the south-west of the city was formed during the Ice Age.

92

Seite 94/95:
Wann kommt der Dampfer, der uns zur Pfaueninsel mit Meierei (oben links), Schloß und Federvieh bringt?

Page 94/95:
When is the steamer coming to take us to Peacock Island with its castle, dairy farm and feathered inhabitants?

Ganz schön abge-
fahren: Der Spree-
park in Treptow lädt
zur Rutschpartie
oder zur luftigen
Rundfahrt.
Und vom Müggel-
turm aus blicken die
Köpenicker auf ihre

Wälder und Gewäs-
ser (unten Mitte und
rechts).

Hold on to your
hats! At the Spree
Amusement Park in
Treptow you can
ride and slide with
the best of them.
And from the
Müggel Tower,
Köpenick residents

can gaze out across
their woods and
lakes (bottom
centre and bottom
right).

Mit Außenbord-
motor oder Wind-
kraft: Der Stolz der
Kladower Freizeit-
kapitäne liegt fest
vertäut.

Outboard motor or
wind-power: the
pride and joy of
Kladow's hobby
sailors is securely
moored.

Spektakel müssen
sein - auch in der
Spandauer Zitadelle.

Back to the Middle
Ages in the Spandau
Citadel.

»Ja, wo laufen sie denn?«: die Galopp-rennbahn in Hoppegarten, östlich der Stadt-grenze, und die Trabrennbahn von Mariendorf (Seite 101).

»Come on, Red Rum!« Horse racing in Hoppegarten, east of the city border and the Mariendorf trotting course (p. 101).

Auf der Köpenicker
Dahme geht's
vorbei am Rathaus
(Seite 102 unten
und oben links), in
dem der legendäre
Hauptmann von
Köpenick das
preußische Prinzip
von Befehl und
Gehorsam unter-
wanderte. Ziel der
Bootspartie könnte
das Schloß auf der
Schloßinsel (oben
rechts) sein.

Sailing past the
town hall (p. 102
bottom and top left)
on the Dahme River
in Köpenick, where
the legendary
captain of Köpenick
ridiculed the
Prussian doctrine
of order and
obedience.
The palace on
Palace Island (top
right) could be the
boot's planned
destination.

Ein »Vierer mit« vor
dem Jagdschloß
Klein-Glienicke und
ein paar »Badegäste
ohne« am Grune-
walder Teufelssee
(unten).

A four »with« in
front of Klein-
Glienicke hunting
lodge and a few
bathers »without«
by the Teufelssee
in Grunewald
(bottom).

Die Woltersdorfer Schleuse (oben) – südöstlich der Stadt – ist ein beliebtes Ziel der Berliner Stern- und Kreisschiffahrt. Zuvor wird der Müggelsee (unten) passiert, genannt »Badewanne der Berliner«.
Seite 106/107: Geschlossene Eisdecke: Daß nicht einmal mehr Eisbrecher eine Fahrrinne für die Flußschiffe freihalten, geschieht höchst selten.

Woltersdorf lock (top) in the southeast of the city is a favourite destination for Berlin's Stern- und Kreisschiffahrt shipping company. The boots first pass the Müggelsee (below), affectionately called »Berlin's bath tub«.
Page 106/107: Frozen solid: it's very rare nowadays that ice-breakers are unable to carve a way through the ice for river transport.

MAUERBLÜMCHEN EROBERN DEN MAUERSTREIFEN

Jetzt können die Mauerblümchen wieder sprießen, ohne von Pestiziden vertilgt zu werden. Der Todesstreifen mußte immer gut geharkt sein, damit potentielle »Republikflüchtlinge« deutliche Spuren hinterlassen. Bäume hatten im Schußfeld sowieso keine Chance.

Die vom einstigen DDR-Verteidigungsminister Heinz Hoffmann als »bestes Grenzssicherungssystem der Welt« gepriesene 165 Kilometer lange Mauer rings um West-Berlin hat sich mancherorts zum Naherholungsgebiet verwandelt. Etwa zwischen Lichterfelde-Süd und Teltow. Dort halten sich Jogger im Laufschritt auf dem alten Patroullienweg fit. Ab und

Lippenbekenntnis: der »Bruderkuß« von Breschnjew und Honecker auf dem zur »East Side Gallery« mutierten Mauerrest.

Lip service: Brezhnev and Honecker's »brother's kiss« on the Wall's »East Side Gallery«.

an lädt sogar eine Parkbank zur Rast. Fast nichts mehr erinnert hier an den zwischen 1961 und 1989 so gut wie unüberwindbaren »antifaschistischen Schutzwall«, zumal eine Bürgerinitiative kräftig aufgeforstet hat. Die Natur erobert sich ihr Terrain zurück, Mauer und Wachtürme sind längst verschwunden. Hier wie fast überall.

Zunächst rückten die »Mauerspechte« mit Hammer und Meißel dem Monstrum zu Leibe, um ein Souvenir

Sprühende Ideen der Graffiti-Kunst auf einem Mauersegment.

Spray-can graffiti art on a section of the Wall.

zu ergattern, dann leistete schweres Gerät ganze Arbeit. Prominentester Rest sind die 1300 Meter der von zahlreichen Künstlern bemalten »East Side Gallery« (Mühlenstraße, Bezirk Friedrichshain). Zwischen dem zuletzt von der Treuhand genutzten alten Reichsluftfahrtministerium und den freigeschaufelten Gestapo-Kellern (Wilhelmstraße, Bezirk Kreuzberg) erinnert ein weiteres Rudiment an die Berliner Vergangenheit. Und an der Bernauer Straße (Wedding) wird ein 70-Meter-Abschnitt als Gedenkstätte gesichert. Doch meist läßt sich der Verlauf der Mauer kaum noch rekonstruieren: Baustellen und neue Straßen haben die Topographie der Stadt total verändert. Leute wie die ehemalige DDR-Bürgerrechtlerin Bärbel Bohley monieren deshalb, daß mit der Mauer »ein Stück deutscher Geschichte« ausradiert worden sei. Berlin-Besucher begnügen sich meist mit einem Rundgang durchs Haus am Checkpoint Charlie, wenn sie etwas über die Situation in der einst geteilten Stadt erfahren wollen. Zur Sammlung am alten Kontrollpunkt Friedrichstraße gehören Fluchtutensilien, die einem noch im nachhinein kalte Mauer-Schauer über den Rücken jagen. Beispielsweise das selbstgebastelte Leichtbauflugzeug mit Trabi-Motor.

WALLFLOWERS TRIUMPH OVER BRICKS AND CONCRETE

The wallflowers along the line of the Berlin Wall can at last grow again without fear of extermination by pesticide. GDR's death strip was always kept well-raked so that potential »Republic refugees« left clear tracks. Trees naturally had no chance in the line of fire.

The 165 kilometres of Wall around West Berlin, praised by former GDR minister of defence Heinz Hoffmann as the »best border security system in the world«, has in some places now become an area of recreation. This is true between Lichterfelde-Süd and Teltow, for example, where joggers keep fit on the old patrol circuit. Occasionally a park bench invites them to take a break. There is hardly anything left to remind us of the almost impenetrable »antifascist protective wall« of 1961 to 1989, torn down by a citizen's action group. Nature is reclaiming her land; the Wall and the watch-towers have long since disappeared.

are the 1,300 metres painted by numerous artists, the East Side Gallery (in the Mühlenstraße, Friedrichshain district). Between the old Air Ministry, last used by Treuhand, and the cellars of the Gestapo headquarters (Wilhelmstraße in the Kreuzberg district), this is one further attestation to Berlin's past. And on the Bernauer Straße (Wedding), a further 70 metre section of Wall has been secured as a memorial. It is generally impossible, however, to reconstruct the Wall's path: building sites and new streets have completely changed the city's topography. People such as the former GDR civil rights campaigner, Bärbel Bohley, lament that a »piece of German history« was eradicated with the Wall.

Visitors to Berlin mostly content themselves with going round the house at Checkpoint Charlie if they wish to find out more about life in the once divided city. The collection at the old Friedrichstraße checkpoint includes escape devices which in retrospect send a cold shiver down your spine. Especially the DIY light aircraft with a Trabant engine.

Noch Nahtstelle zwischen zwei Machtblöcken: der Potsdamer Platz 1988.

Then still a no-man's land separating two world powers: Potsdamer Platz in 1988.

Pink Floyd zelebriert das Rockspektakel »The Wall« auf dem von der Mauer befreiten Potsdamer Platz.

Pink Floyd celebrating a Potsdamer Platz liberated from the Wall with their rock version of »The Wall«.

Here and everywhere else. First the monstrosity was pecked at by »Wall woodpeckers«, armed with hammers and chisels; bigger machines were called in to do the heavy work. The most prominent remains

Was die Uniformierten von Ost und West vor dem Mauerfall trennte, wird jetzt in Tüten verpackt als Souvenir verhökert.

Stumme Zeugen: Jüdische Friedhöfe fordern zum Nachdenken und Meditieren über die Geschichte heraus.

Denk mal! In der Tiergartenstraße 4, wo heute Philharmonie und Kammermusiksaal zum Konzert laden, wurde 1940 nach den Euthanasie-Beschlüssen der erste Massenmord der NS-Zeit organisiert.

What once divided the uniforms of East and West is now packed into bags and disposed of as a souvenir.

Silent witnesses: Jewish cemeteries hypnotise those who enter into reflecting and meditating on past history.

A shuddering thought: in Tiergartenstraße 4, where today concerts are staged in the Philharmonic and the Hall of Chamber Music, the first mass extermination was organised by the Nazis in 1940 after the euthanasia programme was approved.

GESCHICHTSTAFEL

▮▮

um 8000 v. Chr.: Nachweis altsteinzeitlicher Siedlungen im Berliner Raum.

um 1000 v. Chr.: mehrere bronzezeitliche Siedlungen.

um 600 n. Chr.: slawische Besiedelung im Berlin-Brandenburgischen Raum. Slawische Ortsbezeichnungen deuten noch heute darauf hin.

1237: Der Ort Cölln wird erstmals erwähnt. Auf dieses Jahr beziehen sich alle Stadtjubiläen Berlins.

1244: Berlin erstmals erwähnt. Wie in der Region zu dieser Zeit gelebt wurde, veranschaulicht das Museumsdorf Düppel.

1307: Vereinigung von Berlin und Cölln.

1411: Der Nürnberger Burggraf Friedrich VI. aus dem Hause Hohenzollern wird Statthalter in der Mark Brandenburg. 1415 wird er als Friedrich I zum ersten Kurfürsten.

1486: Berlin wird Residenzstadt der Mark Brandenburg.

1539: Kurfürst Joachim II. wechselt zum Protestantismus.

1600: Berlin zählt ca. 12 000 Einwohner.

1640-88: Die nach dem Dreißigjährigen Krieg stark verwüstete Mark erlebt während der Regierungszeit des Großen Kurfürsten Friedrich einen Aufschwung, nicht zuletzt durch den Zuzug der in Frankreich verfolgten Hugenotten. Als Stadterweiterung entsteht die Dorotheenstadt.

1696: Gründung der Akademie der Künste.

1700: Leibniz gründet die Akademie der Wissenschaften.

1701: Kurfürst Friedrich III. krönt sich in Königsberg zum »König in Preußen«.

1726: Gründung des Krankenhauses Charité, heute Universitätsklinikum der Humboldt-Universität.

1740-86: Regierungszeit Friedrichs II., auch Friedrich der Große oder Alter Fritz genannt. Nach dem Siebenjährigen Krieg

entwickelt sich Preußen zur europäischen Großmacht.

um 1800: in Berlin leben mehr als 200 000 Einwohner. Drittgrößte europäische Stadt nach London und Paris.

1806: Napoleon zieht durchs Brandenburger Tor.

1809: Sozialreformen des Freiherrn von Stein.

1810: Gründung der Berliner Universität durch Wilhelm von Humboldt.

1848/49: Märzunruhen, Presse- und Versammlungsfreiheit. Friedrich Wilhelm IV. lehnt die ihm angetragene deutsche Kaiserkrone ab.

1871: Reichsgründung durch Otto von Bismarck, Berlin wird Reichshauptstadt. Wirtschaftlicher Aufschwung (Gründerzeit).

1881: Erste elektrische Straßenbahn in Lichterfelde.

1891: Erste Flugversuche Otto Lilienthals, ebenfalls in Lichterfelde.

1895: Erste Kino-Vorführung durch die Brüder Skladanowsky im Berliner Wintergarten.

1905: Berlin hat fast zwei Millionen Einwohner.

9. November 1918: Ausrufung der Republik zum Ende des Ersten Weltkriegs, Kaiser Wilhelm II. geht ins holländische Exil.

1919: Spartakusaufstand, Straßenkämpfe, Ermordung von Karl Liebknecht und Rosa Luxemburg durch Freikorpssoldaten.

1920: Groß-Berlin wird aus acht Städten, 59 Landgemeinden und 27 Gutsbezirken gebildet und hat nunmehr 3,8 Millionen Einwohner.

1921: Eröffnung der Avus im Grunewald (Automobil-Verkehrs- und -Übungsstraße).

1933: Machtergreifung Adolf Hitlers, Reichstagsbrand, Boykott jüdischer Geschäfte, Bücherverbrennung auf dem Opernplatz.

1936: Olympische Sommerspiele in Berlin.

1937: Albert Speer plant die sogenannte »Reichshauptstadt Germania«.

9. November 1938: Judenverfolgung während der sogenannten »Reichskristallnacht«.

1940: Erste Bombenangriffe während des Zweiten Weltkriegs auf Berlin.

1942: Wannsee-Konferenz über die sogenannte »Endlösung der Judenfrage«.

1943: Propagandaminister Goebbels verkündet im Schöneberger Sportpalast den »totalen Krieg«.

30. April 1945: Selbstmord Adolf Hitlers im Bunker der Reichskanzlei.

2. Mai 1945: Die Wehrmacht kapituliert in Berlin-Karlshorst. Nach dem starken Bombardement sind fast die Hälfte aller Gebäude zerstört, rund 50 000 irreparabel. 75 Millionen Kubikmeter Schutt müssen in den Folgejahren von den Trümmerfrauen beseitigt werden. Berlin hat noch rund zwei Millionen Einwohner. Von ursprünglich rund 60 000 Juden leben noch 7000 in der Stadt. In den Sommermonaten 1945 wird Berlin zur Viersektoren-Stadt.

1948: Die Sowjets verlassen den Alliierten Kontrollrat und die Kommandantura. Letztere ist als Einrichtung der Alliierten die oberste Instanz der Stadtregierung. Nach der Währungsreform in den drei Westsektoren Beginn der rund elfmonatigen, bis zum 12. Mai 1949 dauernden Blockade. Die Westsektoren werden durch die Luftbrücke (»Rosinenbomber«) versorgt.

7. 10. 1949: Gründung der DDR in Ost-Berlin.

17. Juni 1953: Arbeiteraufstand in Ost-Berlin wird mit Hilfe sowjetischer Panzer niedergeschlagen.

1958: Chruschtschow-Ultimatum. Nach dem Willen des Kreml-Chefs soll die Viersektoren-Stadt eine »freie, entmilitarisierte Stadt« werden, die Westsektoren sollen demnach nicht mehr unter dem Schutz der West-Alliierten stehen.

13. August 1961: Nach Massen-Fluchten aus dem Osten Bau der Berliner Mauer.

1963: US-Präsident John F. Kennedy besucht Berlin (»Ick bin ein Börliner«). Passierschein-Abkommen zwischen West- und Ost-Berlin. West-Berliner

können erstmals wieder Verwandte im Ost-Teil besuchen.

1968: West-Berlin ist eines der Zentren der Studentenbewegung.

1971/72: Viermächte-Abkommen und Transit-Abkommen regeln Status-Fragen der Stadt und bringen Erleichterungen im Transitverkehr von und nach Berlin.

1976: Der IX. SED-Parteitag beschließt den Ausbau des Plattenbau-Stadtteils Marzahn im Nordosten.

1979-81: Welle von Hausbesetzungen und Krawallen, vor allem in Kreuzberg.

1987: Beide Stadthälften feiern 750 Jahre Berlin.

7. Oktober 1989: Trotz der über Ungarn rollenden Flucht von DDR-Bürgern wird in Ost-Berlin der 40. Gründungstag der DDR gefeiert. Staatsgast Michail Gorbatschow sagt zum DDR-Staatschef Erich Honecker: »Wer zu spät kommt, den bestraft das Leben.«

18. Oktober 1989: Erich Honecker wird abgesetzt.

9. November 1989: Öffnung der Berliner Mauer. Am 10. und 11. November strömen mehr als eine Million Menschen aus dem Ost-Teil und der DDR nach West-Berlin. Vor dem Schöneberger Rathaus proklamiert Willy Brandt: »Jetzt wächst zusammen, was zusammen gehört.«

31. August 1990: Einigungsvertrag der beiden deutschen Staaten wird im Kronprinzenpalais Unter den Linden unterzeichnet.

20. Juni 1991: Bundestag beschließt die Verlegung von Parlament und Regierung nach Berlin. Bis zum Jahr 2000 soll der Umzug abgeschlossen sein.

September 1994: Die Alliierten Truppen verlassen nach 49jähriger Präsenz Berlin.

Juni/Juli 1995: Reichstags-Verhüllung durch den amerikanisch-bulgarischen Künstler Christo mit rund 100 000 Quadratmeter Spezialgewebe. Anschließend beginnt der Aus- und Umbau des Reichstagsgebäudes für den Deutschen Bundestag.

5. Mai 1996: Volksabstimmung über die Fusion der Länder Berlin und Brandenburg. Die Berliner votieren mehrheitlich dafür, die Brandenburger dagegen, so daß die Länderehe scheitert.

Einst Reichsluftfahrtministerium, bald Finanzministerium: Zwischendurch wurde der NS-Bau an der Wilhelmstraße von der DDR als Haus der Ministerien und von der Treuhand zur Privatisierung des DDR-Volksvermögens genutzt.
Unten: Jüdischer Friedhof.

Once the Imperial Air Ministry of the Third Reich, this Nazi building in Wilhelmstraße will soon be the Ministry of Finance. It has also been home to the GDR House of Ministries and to Treuhand for the privatisation of the GDR's national wealth.
Below: Jurish Cemetary.

Athletisches Imponiergehabe im Dienste der Diktatur: Skulptur am Olympiagelände von 1936.
Unten: Alte Nationalgalerie.

Athletic exhibitionism for the dictatorship: a sculpture in the grounds of the Olympic Stadium from 1936.
Below: Old National Gallery.

CHRONOLOGICAL TABLE

| | | | | | | | | | | | | | | | | | | | | | | | | | | | | | | | | | |

Ca. 8000 BC: First verifiable Palaeolithic settlements in the Berlin area.

Ca. 1000 BC: Several Bronze Age settlements in the Berlin area.

Ca. 600 BC: Slavonic settlements in the Berlin-Brandenburg area. Slavonic place names go back to this period.

1237: Cölln is first mentioned in documents. Berlin's city jubilees are all based on this date.

1244: Berlin is first mentioned in documents. Düppel museum village demonstrates how people in the region lived at this time.

1307: Cölln and Berlin merge.

1411: Frederick VI of Hohenzollern, Burgrave of Nuremberg, is appointed governor of the Brandenburg Marches. In 1415 he becomes the first elector as Frederick I.

1486: Berlin becomes the royal capital of the Brandenburg Marches.

1539: Elector Joachim II converts to Protestantism.

1600: Berlin has ca. 12,000 inhabitants.

1640-88: The Marches, heavily devastated during the Thirty Years' War, experience a boom under the Great Elector Frederick William, not least due to the immigration of the Huguenots, persecuted in their native France. Dorotheenstadt is founded as an extension to the city.

1696: The Academy of Arts is founded.

1700: Leibniz founds the Academy of Sciences.

1701: Elector Frederick III has himself crowned first King of Prussia in Königsberg.

1726: The Charité Hospital is founded, today the Humboldt University Hospital.

1740-86: The reign of Frederick II, also called Frederick the Great or »old Fritz«. After the Seven Years' War, Prussia becomes a European power.

Ca. 1800: More than 200,000 people are living in Berlin. It is the third largest city in Europe after London and Paris.

1806: Napoleon marches through the Brandenburg Gate.

1809: Freiherr von Stein carries out social reform.

1810: Wilhelm von Humboldt founds Berlin University.

1848/49: The March Revolution; after it, freedom of the press and of assembly is granted. Frederick William IV refuses the imperial crown.

1871: Otto von Bismarck founds the German Reich. Berlin becomes imperial capital. Germany experiences a period of economic boom (Gründerzeit).

1881: The first electric tramway is opened in Lichterfelde.

1891: Otto Lilienthal makes his first attempts at flying, also in Lichterfelde.

1895: First cinema showing by the Skladanovsky brothers in Berlin's winter garden.

1905: Berlin has almost 2 million inhabitants.

9th November, 1918: The Weimar Republic is called into being at the end of the First World War. On 10th November, William II (»Kaiser Bill«) goes into exile in The Netherlands.

1919: Spartacus uprising and street fighting; soldiers from the volunteer corps murder Karl Liebknecht and Rosa Luxemburg.

1920: Greater Berlin comprises eight towns, 59 rural districts and 27 estates, and now has 3.8 million inhabitants.

1921: Avus (Germany's first car racing circuit) is opened in Grunewald.

1933: Adolf Hitler comes to power, followed by the burning of the Reichstag, a boycott of Jewish shops, and book burnings on Opernplatz.

1936: The 11th Olympic Games is held in Berlin.

1937: Albert Speer designs Germania, »capital of the Reich«.

9th November, 1938: Persecution of Jews during Reichskristallnacht (Crystal Night).

1940: Berlin suffers its first air raids during the Second World War.

1942: Wannsee Conference on the »final solution to the Jewish problem«.

1943: Propaganda minister Goebbels proclaims »total war« from the Schöneberg sports stadium.

30th April, 1945: Hitler commits suicide in his bunker at the Reichskanzelei.

2nd May, 1945: The German army capitulates in Berlin-Karlshorst. After heavy bombardments, almost half of the city's buildings have been destroyed, 50,000 of them beyond repair. 75 million cubic metres of rubble are cleared away by the Trümmerfrauen in the next few years. Berlin now only has two million inhabitants. Of the 60,000 Jews in Berlin, only 7,000 have survived. In the summer months of 1945, Berlin is divided into four sectors.

1948: The Soviets leave the Allied Command Council and headquarters. The latter, set up by the Allies, is the top level of authority in the ravaged city. After monetary reform is instigated in the three west sectors, the eleven-month Berlin Blockade begins, lasting until 12th May, 1949. The legendary Western airlift flies supplies in to the west sectors.

7th October, 1949: The German Democratic Republic is founded in East Berlin.

17th June, 1953: A worker's revolt in East Berlin is crushed with the help of Soviet tanks.

1958: Khrushchev's ultimatum. The head of the Kremlin wants to make four-zone Berlin a »free, demilitarised city«, whereby the west sectors are no longer protected by the Allies.

13th August, 1961: Erection of the Berlin Wall after mass emigration from the East.

1963: US president John F. Kennedy visits Berlin (»Ik bin ein Burlinner«). Permit agreement signed between East and West Berlin. West Berlin residents can see relatives in the East again for the first time.

1968: West Berlin is one of the centres of the student movement.

1971/72: The Four Powers Agreement on Berlin regulates Berlin's status quo and relieves transit problems in traffic to and from Berlin.

1976: The 9th SED party conference decides to extend the concrete jungle of the Marzahn district in the north-east of the city.

1979-81: Berlin experiences a wave of riots and squats, especially in Kreuzberg.

1987: Both halves of the city celebrate 750 years of Berlin.

7th October, 1989: Despite the flood of GDR emigrants escaping to the West through Hungary, East Berlin celebrates 40 years of the GDR. State guest Mikhail Gorbachov tells the GDR head of state, Erich Honecker: »Life punishes those who come too late.«

18th October, 1989: Erich Honecker is removed from office.

9th November, 1989: The Berlin Wall is opened. On the 10th and 11th November, more than a million people stream into West Berlin from the east of the city and the GDR. In front of the Schöneberg town hall, Willy Brandt announces: »All that was once one should now reunite.«

31st August, 1990: The unification treaty is signed by both German states in the Crown Prince's Palace in Unter den Linden.

20th June, 1991: The Bundestag decides to move parliament and the seat of government to Berlin. The move is to be effected by the year 2000.

September, 1994: After 49 years, Allied troops leave Berlin.

June/July, 1995: American-Bulgarian artist Christo wraps the Reichstag with ca. 100,000 square metres of special fabric. Once the project is finished, major rebuilding work is started on the Reichstag for the German Bundestag.

5th May, 1996: A plebiscite is held on the fusion of the states of Berlin and Brandenburg. The Berliners vote in favour, the people of Brandenburg against the proposal, blocking the marriage of the two states.

Die Baustelle als illuminiertes Happening: Kunstspektakel von Gerhard Merz am Potsdamer Platz im Sommer 1996.

The building site as illuminated happening: Gerhard Merz's art show on Potsdamer Platz in the summer of 1996.

REGISTER

Die Deutsche Bibliothek - CIP-Einheitsaufnahme

Berlin / Volker Oesterreich; Jürgen Henkelmann
Würzburg : Stürtz, 1996
ISBN 3-8003-0784-7
NE: Oesterreich, Volker; Henkelmann, Jürgen

Bildnachweis
S. 18 unten und S. 19 oben:
© Christo und Jeanne-Claude, Verhüllter Reichstag,
Berlin 1971-95/ W. Volz/ Bilderberg

Alle Rechte vorbehalten
© 1996 Stürtz Verlag GmbH, Würzburg
© Fotografie: Jürgen Henkelmann
Text: Volker Oesterreich
Übersetzung: Rapid Communication, Ruth Chitty
Grafik: Sabine Simon, Marktheidenfeld
Repro: Fischer Repro Technik, Frankfurt
Satz: Fotosatz Richard, Kitzingen
Druck und Verarbeitung: Universitätsdruckerei H. Stürtz,
Würzburg
Printed in Germany
ISBN 3-8003-0784-7